T0316271

CHAWTON HOUSE LIBRARY SERIES

WOMEN'S TRAVEL WRITINGS IN IBERIA

CONTENTS OF THE EDITION

Chawton House Library Series: Women's Travel Writings

Series Editors: Stephen Bending and Stephen Bygrave

Titles in this Series

Women's Travel Writings in Revolutionary France
Women's Travel Writings in Italy
Women's Travel Writings in Post-Napoleonic France

Forthcoming Titles

Women's Travel Writings in North Africa and the Middle East
Women's Travel Writings in Scotland

WOMEN'S TRAVEL WRITINGS IN IBERIA

Volume 1
Marianne Baillie, *Lisbon in the Years 1821, 1822, and 1823* (1824)
Volume I

EDITED BY

José Ruiz Mas

Routledge
Taylor & Francis Group

LONDON AND NEW YORK

First published 2013 by Pickering & Chatto (Publishers) Limited

Published 2016 by Routledge
2 Park Square, Milton Park, Abingdon, Oxon OX14 4RN
711 Third Avenue, New York, NY 10017, USA

Routledge is an imprint of the Taylor & Francis Group, an informa business

BRITISH LIBRARY CATALOGUING IN PUBLICATION DATA

Women's travel writings in Iberia. – (Chawton House library series. Women's
travel writings)
1. Iberian Peninsula – Description and travel. 2. Travelers' writings, English –
Iberian Peninsula. 3. Women travelers – Iberian Peninsula – History – 19th
century – Sources.
I. Series II. Demetriou, Eroulla editor of compilation. III. Ruiz Mas, Jose
editor of compilation. IV. Lopez-Burgos, Ma. Antonia (Maria Antonia) editor
of compilation. V. Baillie, Marianne, c. 1795–1831. Lisbon. VI. Chatterton,
Georgiana, Lady, 1806–1876. Pyrenees. VII. Ellis, Sarah Stickney, 1799–1872.
Summer and winter in the Pyrenees.
914.6'0472'082-dc23

ISBN-13: 978-1-85196-647-9 (set)

Typeset by Pickering & Chatto (Publishers) Limited

CONTENTS

GENERAL INTRODUCTION

During the nineteenth century, travelling in Spain and Portugal was still a risky business, indeed it was a real adventure. Once in the Peninsula, many felt the irresistible need to put pen to paper and depict the events which took place during their travels with detailed remarks and observations.[1] The main intention of most travellers was to unveil the transcendental soul of these indomitable lands, which, although backward compared to other European countries, offered picturesque and colourful landscapes, impressive architecture of all periods and unforgettable experiences. But most of all, they were countries which were considered 'different'. Travel books were widely read, popular at social gatherings and all in all proved to be a booming business for many publishers whenever they included 'Iberian literary topics'.[2]

The first two decades of the nineteenth century were dominated by male travellers' accounts written in connection with the Peninsular War (1808–14). A number of titles give eyewitness accounts of major military campaigns in the Iberian Peninsula. This war had brought thousands of reluctant French and British military men to Spain and Portugal and had contributed to putting both Iberian countries on the map, as the war exploits were duly written up as memoirs by some of those participating in the military campaigns. Some Romantic poets and scholars promoted the idea of Spain and Portugal as heroic countries which rebelled against tyranny and the loss of freedom to a foreign power, Napoleon's France. The heteropias of Spain, Portugal, Spanish America and Brazil functioned powerfully in the cultural grammar of the Romantic era in Britain. The Peninsular War and the Wars of Independence of the Spanish colonies and the Portuguese colony of Brazil constituted key periods of Anglo-Iberian Romantic relations.[3] In America a Spanish trail had already been blazed by George Ticknor, who travelled to Spain to learn the language and prepare himself for a chair of Spanish at Harvard, and by the short story writer and future diplomat, Washington Irving. Partly through their influence, American circles had begun to take a greater interest in all things Spanish, especially after Irving's *Tales of The Alhambra* (1832). In Britain Lord Byron helped to popularize Spain and Portugal with his *Don Juan* and *Childe Harold's Pilgrimage* but other Romantic poetic and historical works also contributed: Felicia Hemans's 'The Domestic Affections', 'England and Spain' and 'The Abencerrage'; Robert Southey's 'Roderick', *History of Brazil* and *History of the Peninsular War*; Walter Scott's 'Don Julian'; Mary Leman Grimstone's 'Zayda'; Barry Conwall's 'Diego de Montilla'; Terence MacMahon Hughes's 'Iberia Won'; Lord Porchester's 'The Moor' and George Croly's 'Sebastian', to name but a few.

English Romanticism brought another type of traveller to Iberian lands. During the first decades of the nineteenth century, Spain was conceived as one of the most romantic and exotic countries in the western world, but together with Portugal, they were also considered two of the most backward and dangerous in Europe. Banditry and thieving were rampant on Spain's country roads and in the whereabouts of *ventas* owing to the recent Peninsular War, the first Carlist War, political and social insecurity and the generalized corruption of the politicians under the absolutist King Fernando VII. Constant dirt, filthiness and a chronic laziness were Portugal's main enemies according to foreign eyes. The Portuguese administration had come to a complete collapse due to the French occupation of their country during the Peninsular War and there was an intense political apathy in Portugal, especially during the first part of the reign of King D. João VI. The Royal Family had been absent, as they had left the country and settled in Brazil during the aforementioned conflict and did not feel too anxious to leave their Brazilian Eden until the early 1820s, when the monarch was forced to accept a liberal constitution imposed on him by the peaceful 1820 Porto Revolution.

After the Peninsular War, the turbulent pre-railway years (1820–50) both in Spain and Portugal marked a highpoint in Peninsular travel writing which has never been equalled. British and American writers such as George Borrow, Richard Ford, Alexander Slidell MacKenzie, Henry Wadsworth Longfellow and Benjamin Disraeli, to list some of the best-known names, traversed the Iberian Peninsula's regions taking due note of their findings and rejoicing whenever faced with Spain and Portugal's backwardness and primitiveness, ideal elements which gave a sense of adventure and spark to their accounts.

Although a trip south of the Pyrenees after having undertaken the learned European Grand Tour was not considered to be exactly fashionable or stylish, it was, nonetheless, fully in keeping with the vogue for Orientalism that had enthralled the Continent. Tales of lascivious gypsy girls, gallant highwaymen, menacing Carlists, exotic and passionate dances, strange and superstitious customs that were reminiscent of Arab times of old, pagan and bloody bullfights, inquisitorial rites performed by sinister Spanish and Portuguese Catholic monks, public executions or auto-da-fés, descriptions of decayed gothic-like castles, cemeteries and secretive monasteries and convents and Oriental ghost palaces abounded in travel accounts in the nineteenth century. The use of southern settings such as Spain and Portugal (as well as the south of France and Italy) in many Gothic novels of the classical period from the mid-eighteenth century to the first third of the nineteenth century implied that this background was an integral feature of Gothic fiction. The exploration of southern European scenery can be directly connected to the anti-Catholic, political and cultural prejudices strongly held by the British travellers against Roman Catholic countries. Some travelling authors had directly experienced this scenery which they promptly incorporated and recreated in their novels. Those novelists who had not travelled to the places which they depicted in their works resorted to stereotypes following narrative conventions as well as descriptions of remote and unknown ruins, decaying castles, monasteries and cemeteries in southern settings and secretive conversations with invariably beautiful nuns with dark, enchanting and enigmatic eyes who had been persuaded by their own families to be secluded for life among the four walls of prison-like convents. It is in the south where we can find the Catholicism/politics symbiosis embodied in the 'other'. The south in Gothic fiction plays an active part in the English Protestant imagination in the eighteenth and nineteenth centuries.

Although male travellers wrote most of their travel accounts on the Peninsula during the first half of the nineteenth century, there were also a number of courageous and intrepid women who offered valuable testimonies of their adventures in Peninsular lands. Their travel accounts are full of incisive criticism and acute descriptions of society. They judge each and every aspect of the different ranks of the Spanish and Portuguese societies, visiting palaces and ancestral houses, convents and monasteries. All were of noble birth, ladies of lineage who were rich, spirited, educated and usually well-read. Their remarks and observations have a continuous aspect of proximity with everyday life; they are more concerned with small details and with more intense observations of daily routines. If as a general rule in men's narratives we find a constant and confessed interest in institutional aspects, women travellers pay more attention to social attitudes and their scenarios.

Indeed, among the avalanche of travellers who started to include Spain and/or Portugal in their travel aspirations in the nineteenth century there were some women who saw travelling as a way of defiantly combating the existing male-oriented rules of pre-Victorian times. The majority of these women had to struggle for recognition in a society which systematically objected to any type of physical and psychological independence from men and from man-made social conventions. A sense of liberty which was only obtainable through travel to the remotest lands (the Iberian Peninsula was still considered as such) was frowned upon, unless they did so with their husbands or other male relatives. Few of these women escaped misunderstanding and ill-intentioned remarks about their suspiciously free natures. Early nineteenth-century Spain was visited only by the bravest, such as Lady Holland, who travelled in the country during or just after the Peninsular War. However, during the reign of Isabel II (1833–68) and the subsequent decades, the number of women travellers grew dramatically and included Caroline Elizabeth Cushing, the Marquess of Londonderry, Maria Witson, E. M. Grosvenor, two anonymous women writers, I. F. Romer, Dora Quillinan, Lady Tenison, E. Murray, S. Dunbar, H. T. Allen, M. Eyre, Mrs Byrne, Lady E. Herbert, Mathilda B. B. Edwards, Mrs M. Tollemache, Mrs C. H. Ramsay, A. J. Harvay, M. C. Jackson, E. Burges, Kate Field, Lisbeth C. Strahan, L. Howard-Vyse, Frances Elliot, Mrs P. Crawford, Lizzie W. Champney, Jane Leck, Mrs E. R. Whitwell and Margaret Thomas. The presence or absence of these women travellers in Spain at different periods of the turbulent nineteenth century is revealing of the varying perception of the country as a troubled land that could be visited or avoided depending on the circumstances. When the country was deeply immersed in political or social turmoil, or undergoing a civil or international war such as the Peninsular War or the Carlist Wars, the Espartero–Narváez tug of war for power during the 1840s, or when under the threat of José María el Tempranillo's rule in Andalusia in the 1830s, it is evident that foreign women visitors steered clear of Spain. Indeed, up to the 1840s the number of women visitors is rather meagre. However, when Spain began to enjoy rare periods of political tranquility (despite the three Carlist Wars, which scarcely affected Andalusia, the region which attracted the largest number of visitors), such as General Narváez's peaceful ten-year government in the 1840s and 1850s, the short-lived but tranquil reign of Alfonso XII (1875–85) and the infant reign of Alfonso XIII through his mother's regency (1885–1902), the number of globetrotters from high walks of life multiplied considerably, including women travellers. Portugal also received her fair share of English-speaking women writers throughout the nineteenth century, most of them from the 1820s onwards, such as Clarissa Trant (author of the then unknown *The Journal of Clarissa Trant 1800–1832*, published in 1925), Marianne Baillie, Julia H. S. Pardoe, E. M. Grosvenor, Dora Quillinan, E. Stuart Wortley, S. Dunbar, Catherine Charlotte Jackson and Jane Leck.

From the 1870s onwards, as each year passed and travelling became easier and more comfortable, a veritable invasion of tourists descended upon Spain and Portugal, especially the former. The number of travel accounts, most of which were extraordinarily similar, swelled and their literary quality reached rock bottom, as they all repeated the same clichés and the same standard descriptions of the sights seen: the never-ending religious bigotry of the Spanish and Portuguese, a bullfight, a visit to the Prado Museum and to the Alhambra, the confessed distrust for the odd peasant who was 'no doubt' a brigand or a smuggler in disguise, and so forth. Two factors contributed considerably to this larger flow of English-speaking men and women travellers in the Iberian Peninsula: the railway's deployment, making the routes between the main towns more comfortable and almost devoid of unpleasant surprises, and in the case of Spain, the proven efficiency of the Guardia Civil, created in the 1840s.[4] In the 1870s almost all travel in Spain could be accomplished by rail, and the tourists, although not yet as numerous as in other fashionable European lands such as Germany, Switzerland, France and Italy (still part of a now decaffeinated Grand Tour), could nevertheless be counted by the tens of thousands. The selling of guidebooks (Murray's, Baedeker's, O'Shea's) was already a booming business for any publisher with an eye set on travel.

Three British women writers have been chosen to represent women's travel writing in the Iberian Peninsula in the first half of the nineteenth century: Mrs Marianne Baillie, an aspiring poet who was forced to spend two and a half dreadful years in Portugal, the result of which was her *Lisbon in the Years 1821, 1822, and 1823* (1824); Mrs Sarah Ellis, a well-known Protestant ideologist and missionary who wrote numerous books about the middle class and aristocratic women's important role in the new Victorian society, and was also a reluctant traveller to southern lands (the French Pyrenees) while accompanying her ailing husband, which resulted in her travel account *Summer and Winter in the Pyrenees* (1841); and Lady Henrietta Georgiana Chatterton, an idle but cultivated invalid aristocrat who, in spite of her constant health problems, wrote *The Pyrenees with Excursions into Spain* (1843) after her visit, again for reasons of health, to the southern areas of France close to the Pyrenees, which included three excursions to the beautiful and picturesque wilderness of the Catalan and Basque valleys on the other side of the French frontier.

These three women travellers had certain features in common. The most clearly visible one is their deep patriotism and nostalgia for their country when abroad. England for them was the perfect epitome of civilization and progress and therefore they did not cease to express their homesickness for their comfortable homes. All these women also travelled south either against their will or stayed in the Peninsula as little as possible. Mrs Baillie was overjoyed to leave Portugal as soon as her husband was given leave to do so. Mrs Ellis assures her readers that the best thing about travelling was the pleasure of returning home; Lady Chatterton, a compulsive traveller in search of her lost health, was also always happy to return to England. Another issue of importance is their strong Anglican/Protestant faith, set in constant contrast to what they saw as the superstitious and illogical Catholic practices of the Peninsular countries (although this is less evident in the writings of Lady Chatterton, who converted to Catholicism at the end of her life).

None of these three women travellers could be seen as models of vocational intrepid travellers in search of new lands or independence from men's tyranny. Mrs Baillie, faithful to her condition as a wife, accompanied her husband to Portugal when he was charged with a certain unexplained political mission by their protector Lord Chichester (to whom her book is dedicated); Mrs Ellis accompanied her ailing husband, the celebrated missionary and experienced travel writer Rev. William Ellis, to the Béarn and the Pau area, in the south of France, when he was suffering health problems (probably a depression); she would have preferred the more fashionable Switzerland, but put on a brave face and travelled to Pau and the French Pyrenees for her husband's convalescence. Mrs Ellis's attention was at all times devoted to her husband's well-being, happiness, accompaniment and health, behaving always as the perfect spouse. In the case of Lady Chatterton, an invalid suffering from 'low spirits' since her parents and aunt had died, she was always accompanied by Sir William Abraham Chatterton. She would often even leave the responsibility of the excursions in the French Pyrenees to her husband, who would undertake them alone and would later describe to her the landscapes contemplated and the impressions felt which she would then rephrase to make them part of her travel account. Her health-seeking journeys to the south did not cure her and she found this disappointing. Many times she was happy just to see the four walls of a hotel and to experience the luxury of staying there.

Their respective journeys or stays in Spain or Portugal were either for the shortest possible time or even non-existent. Mrs Ellis did not once set foot on Spanish soil. Lady Chatterton was the only one to express some enjoyment while visiting France and Spain (although she was often not in the mood for sightseeing), but her low spirits prevented her from moving too far into Spain (the furthest she travelled was San Sebastian) or too far from the comfort of her French headquarters. Mrs Baillie and Mrs Ellis evidenced an overt distrust towards the Peninsular countries, which they described as semi-civilized and which they always regarded as inferior to Britain and British things in all respects. Even if Mrs Ellis did not cross the French–Spanish border a single time, she voices her prejudiced opinions of the wretched Spaniards she saw in France: shepherds, mule drivers, bandits (she says) and exiles.

Another common characteristic that they shared was that while abroad, being members or aspiring members of the upper classes, these three women were aided continuously by a train of hired local and British servants, guides and governesses. Lady Chatterton was even carried in a litter throughout some excursions. Mrs Baillie and Mrs Ellis had an army of servants in charge of the house chores and, in the case of Mrs Ballie, in charge of the care of her two children. The three of them also had sufficient economic means to lead comfortable lives abroad for a long period of time, either in hotels or in rented mansions. They tried to mingle with the higher social, political and intellectual spheres of society and showed this off as often as they could. Though fairly or highly cultivated, they were easy prey to the prejudices and distrust that the British felt for decadent southern countries such as Portugal and Spain. These women travellers cannot be said to be the best examples of intrepid and independent travellers in search of opening new routes for civilization's welfare and for women's rights.

Let us now concentrate on these female writers' opinions of the Iberian Peninsula as expressed in their travel accounts. Marianne Baillie (née Wathen, c. 1795–1830) resided in Portugal for two and a half years in the early 1820s because her husband was sent there for work reasons.[5] As a way of letting off steam and passing abundant hours of forced leisure, she wrote a series of sixty-five letters to her mother in England which constitute *Lisbon in the Years 1821, 1822, and 1823* (1824). The collected letters (most of them lacking information about herself as a wife or mother) inform the reader of her lonely stay in Lisbon (which she hated for its horrid odours and lack of cleanliness) and in Sintra (a quieter and healthier residential area for the high classes). She loathed her life of solitude and boredom, especially during the first half of her Portuguese stay, and suffered Portugal's backwardness and generalized filthiness as a consequence of the devastated state in which the Peninsular War had left the country. She abhorred anything Portuguese: its people, their apparent religious bigotry, ignorance and ugliness (the only exception to this latter trait being the unfortunate nuns who, despite their attractive eyes, were forcedly secluded against their will in the Catholic prison-like convents). She scarcely even managed to learn the language. She only used English and French to her acquaintances and servants and tried hard only to mingle with the aristocracy, the high army ranks and the diplomacy, both Portuguese and British. Her chronic boredom was combated by learning how to play the guitar, writing a few poems (which would later be published in *Trifles in Verse* [1825]), drawing, going on some excursions to convents (she seemed to have a soft spot for them) and her friendship with the Countess de Anadia, an outgoing Portuguese aristocrat who introduced her to the social atmosphere of the highest classes and the diplomacy. Her anti-Catholicism oozes continually from her pages (probably to reaffirm her Englishness abroad) and her homesickness for England is the recurrent topic in her reflections and observations of Portugal in her letters. She nevertheless took advantage of her stay in the country to narrate the complex political situation in which Portugal was immersed in the early 1820s, making her first-hand account of the political situation in Portugal a historical document of prime value. She witnessed the arrival at Lisbon of King D. João VI from Brazil, the disagreements of the different members of the royal family with the imposed constitution and the newly-proclaimed Cortes, and especially the discord between the king and his wife D. Carlota Joaquina, and between the king and his sons D. Pedro (the regent of Brazil and later proclaimed emperor of the South-American ex-colony) and D. Miguel, aspirer to an absolutist throne of Portugal. She also witnessed the burial of the Queen Mother D. Maria I, the revolt of Prince D. Miguel for the abolishment of the liberal constitution (the 'Vilafrancada'), the British and French diplomatic struggle to try to influence the king's political decisions, the hysterical reaction of the Portuguese people after the miraculous apparition of the Virgin of the Buraca in a cave near Lisbon, the first political and military steps taken towards the independence of Brazil and the Portuguese administration's first reactions. The day when Mrs Baillie received the letter granting the couple (and their two small children) permission to return home to England was probably one of the happiest days of her life. Only at the end of her two-and-a-half-year stay in Portugal did she begin to enjoy the country and understand some of its mores; and she at least bid the country a friendly farewell: 'Never shall I forget *some* pleasant days we have passed here; nor the distinguished kindness we have received from *certain of* its inhabitants' (our italics) (vol. 2, p. 257, page numbers refer to this Pickering & Chatto edition).

Mrs Sarah Ellis, née Stickney (1799–1872), daughter of a tenant farmer, became a prolific defender of the social mission of the English middle-class and middle upper-class women of the post-Romantic age, as is demonstrated in her numerous conduct books on the role of women in English society.[6] Mrs Ellis contributed enormously to the preservation of the current *status quo* by writing eloquently about women's duties towards both family and country from an overtly Protestant perspective. Most of her books were bestsellers in her day. Through them she encouraged the conformation of women's strong moral position in society as the main source of education and support for men under a woman's influence, namely husbands, sons, brothers, man-servants and so forth. Mrs Ellis incessantly wrote conduct books for Victorian women about the domestic, religious, moral and managerial role of the rising middle class, always from a missionary point of view. The influence of women within the Victorian home was to be unquestionable, an idea to which Mrs Ellis's writings as well as other conduct books and women novels contributed enormously ever since Hannah More published *Hints towards Forming the Character of a Young Princess* (1805), where the numerous educational, moral and domestic occupations in which women should be involved were outlined. Mrs Ellis's *Summer and Winter in the Pyrenees* (1841) reflects a didacticism which is characteristic of her writings, in line with most of her prior and future observations on the subtle but relevant role of women in English society. The opinions expressed in her personal diary and later transported to this travel account anticipate the views expressed later in her ensuing moralistic conduct books. At the very time when Mrs Ellis was travelling in the south of France, her book *Women of England* (1839) was in the process of becoming a bestseller, and her subsequent equally successful sequels, *Daughters of England* (1842), *Wives of England* (1843) and *Mothers of England* (1843) were published only a few years after her residence abroad. She wrote incessantly about the domestic, religious, moral and management roles of the middle-class Victorian woman, but she also dedicated some passages to the behaviour of English women travellers when abroad. Travelling, except when it is done for health reasons, could not be recommendable, she wrote in her travel account, especially for people whose minds were not yet solidly formed. She affirms, 'there is great danger in bringing young persons of unformed character, abroad' (vol. 5, p. 407), and goes on to say that 'The more we are inured in early life to the performance of practical duty, the stronger will be our moral basis, the more consistent our religious life' (p. 407). The reader receives the impression that she is implying that the less a woman travels, the better. It is no coincidence that the motto employed under the book title is 'I have no pleasure that will compare with going abroad, excepting one – returning home', taken from Inglis's *Spain in 1830* (1831). Indeed, Mrs Ellis was of the opinion that young women such as daughters who were easy prey to the lure of adventure and leisurely travel should not miss not travelling.

Mrs Ellis never set foot in Spain. She hardly knew anything about the country or showed any special interest in it. She was staying in France and was not at all obliged to visit the Iberian Peninsula. Proof of this is that when she had the chance, she did not cross the Spanish–French border, and the little she did write about the other side of the Pyrenees was mostly contaminated by the ill-informed clichés that abounded in British people's minds and works of the nineteenth century, presumably as a result of the widespread anti-Spanish and anti-Catholic tradition among the British Protestants (she and her husband were staunch Protestants) which dated back to the sixteenth century. However, despite the fact that Mrs Ellis did not cross the Spanish frontier a single time (indeed, she did not have to), her view of the Spaniards and a number of things Spanish were frequently expressed in her travel account. Her perception of Spain and her depictions of the country and its people in *Summer and Winter in the Pyrenees* were nevertheless limited to her superficial impressions of the Spaniards who crossed the Spanish–French natural border of the Pyrenees for a variety of reasons. She admitted to being partly influenced by her reading of the odd travel account on Spain such as Inglis's *Spain in 1830* because this book dedicated its first part to exploring and describing the Spanish western part of the Pyrenees. She did not admit, however, to having copied whole fragments of factual information on the Béarn area from local books.

The Spaniards who Mrs Ellis had the opportunity to observe in an overt attitude of sincere curiosity, and with a mixture of admiration and rejection, belonged to three different types. They were either groups of political exiles, about whom she writes little, for she does not seem to be familiar or concerned with anything that goes further than the label of 'political turbulence' in Spain; or they were members of the numerous troops of 'wild-looking' shepherds and mule drivers who crossed the border for reasons of trade, always accompanied by their beasts; or they were health-seekers of a poorer class than the other European foreigners who patronized the fashionable Pyrenean health resorts. According to Mrs Ellis,

the Spaniards were more than content with having access to the spas of lesser quality in the Pau area: 'More interesting to me were some other fountains of health
[at Cauterets], higher up the valley, either too humble or too distant to be visited
by any but the poorest class, and those were chiefly Spaniards' (vol. 5, p. 358).
Ellis disliked Cauterets precisely because it was full of Spanish health-seekers and
described the village as the strangest-looking place in the Pyrenees, 'being almost
filled with Spaniards, to whose exclusive use one set of its many baths is appropriated ... with the apparent poverty, and filth of the Spaniards, [who] rendered the
place by no means agreeable for a protracted stay' (vol. 5, p. 350).

Some allegedly characteristic features are constantly repeated by Mrs Ellis
in her visual description of the Spaniards: their wild looks, their poverty and
filthiness, their peculiar clothes, always consisting of a woollen mantle slung on
one of their shoulders, and their majestic deportment, the only remnant of a
once-proud race. The detailed description of the Spanish peasants' clothes takes
up most of the space dedicated to them, a fact which proves her scant knowledge
of Spanish history and contemporary affairs. She never exchanged a single word
with a Spaniard as far as can be gleaned from her travel account. An excellent
example of her ignorance of Spanish issues is her disinterest in explaining the
turbulent political situation in the neighbouring country that provoked the exile
of a good number of Spaniards. As for her blatant lack of knowledge of Spanish
history, her ludicrous hypothesis on the origin of the Basque language in the
south of France is simply unbeatable (vol. 5, p. 339).

Having reached the last villages of the French side of the Pyrenees, Mrs Ellis
believes she had travelled far enough south. She finds that the heat is already
excessive; uncleanliness and filth are persistent in the most southern areas of
France, especially those that are nearest to Spain; the 'race' of these 'semi-civilized countries' (meaning the south of France and Spain), she says, is more and
more decadent as one heads closer towards the south. To leap over the Spanish
frontier does not even cross her mind, as the worst features of 'southerness', she
seems to suspect, would come to the very worst there. After visiting the skirts of
the French Pyrenees she had had enough. Her belief in southern spiritual and
physical decay seems confirmed when she sights large troops of Spanish mule
drivers, most probably banditti, she adds, and wretched Cagots who inhabit the
area that is closest to Spain, the country that best epitomizes 'southerness'. She
has an (unidentified) friend, she says, who, after a two or three-hour ride on
the Spanish side of the border, kept her satisfactorily informed of the decadence
and misery that he could see on the other side of the Pyrenees, the last frontier
of civilization (vol. 5, pp. 376–7). For Mrs Ellis the first signs of the 'south' are
already perceivable once Bordeaux is left behind on the way to Pau: here the
French peasant begins to look like a Spaniard, or what she believes a Spaniard
should look like (wearing a beret-like cap and a cloak thrown over one shoul-

der). Anything that comes from the south (that is, from Spain) is to be distrusted, she implies. In fact, even the only uncomfortable wind in the Pyrenees happens to come from Spain: 'The only time when the air was oppressive, was during the prevalence of a south, or Spanish wind' (vol. 5, p. 135), she states. And one also had to be wary of the Arabs coming from Spain throughout French history: 'It is the opinion of many [historians], that the latter [the chateau of Pau] was built as a place of defence against the incursions of the Saracens from Spain' (vol. 5, p. 159). After all, was it not, according to the author, the Spanish Muslims who had initiated trade with the south of France? 'At the time when he [Gaston III] flourished, a very extensive traffic, entirely monopolized by the Saracens, was carried on with the east by the way of Oleron [France] and Jaca [Spain]' (vol. 5, p. 200), she wrote of the antecedents of Spanish–French commercial relations. Nothing good could come from Spain. This country, she claimed, exported wild-looking men that could well be banditti carrying or wearing 'a vast variety of things, that looked not only foreign, but suspicious, to our unaccustomed eyes' (vol. 5, p. 241). The demonization of all things southern reaches even the alleged famed beauty of southern women. If southern women are widely thought to be attractive (she assures the reader that she had enough proof of this while in Bordeaux), she is disappointed to find that this was not the case with those nearest to the Spanish frontier. Indeed, she found that the closer she came to Spain, the uglier the women became. For Mrs Ellis, the equation is clear: 'southern woman' (even if she is French) equals 'Spanish woman' (disappointingly ugly, as this does not comply with the cliché that she was expecting to confirm) (vol. 5, pp. 42–3). At long last, she manages to see real Spaniards, and not French peasants resembling Spaniards. In the human fauna that she comes across in the Parc at Pau (a local place of social intercourse), she notices that the largest bulk of foreigners are Spaniards, naturally dressed in the manner which she had anticipated at Bordeaux: 'with their long dark cloaks, lined with red, and gracefully thrown over one shoulder' (vol. 5, p. 50). She nevertheless dedicates a few words with a slight tone of sympathy to those Spanish political refuges residing at Pau who, she says, were no doubt members of the high society in their native country but who were now obliged to make a poor living by carrying out jobs below their class (vol. 5, pp. 136–7). The Spanish mule drivers who Ellis incessantly encounters at fairs and on roads – 'troops of wild-looking Spaniards [who] rather startled me' – have their outfits described by Mrs Ellis with a generous display of details. She praises the beautiful mules that the Spaniards trade with; however, 'the Spaniards by whom they [the mules] are accompanied, are the most striking and picturesque objects [she has] ever seen'. The physical features described by the author would be the ones very probably employed to describe any member of the southern races: 'abject-looking', 'lean', 'tall', 'thin sharp features', 'frizzled brown hair', 'dirty complexions', 'sharp sunken eyes', 'shrivelled skins', 'mean features' or 'brown curling hair'. Mrs Ellis's perception

xx   *Women's Travel Writings in Iberia, Volume 1*

of the southern-featured Spaniards, a proud people now in decadence, conveys a mixed feeling of attraction and rejection. The mysterious inhabitants of the Peninsula south of the French Pyrenees constitute a singular post-Romantic blend of uncleanliness and dignity, ugliness and elegance, poverty and nobility, Arab-looking human types and Christians (vol. 5, p. 351).

Henrietta Georgiana Marcia Lascelles Chatterton (née Iremonger, 1806–76) was not born an aristocrat,[7] but was a well-educated only child who had had a French maid and an Italian governess, thus allowing her to learn French and Italian from an early age during her happy childhood. The intense grief caused by her aunt's death and eventually by the death of her parents was probably, she wrote, the cause of her bad health, the 'low spirits' from which she suffered so much. And, what is worse, she did not feel that her voyages to the south, where she had placed many of her hopes for recovery, had helped much to improve her health. At the age of seventeen, in 1824, she married Sir William Abraham Chatterton, and soon after they travelled in Ireland and Italy. In 1837, her first novel *Aunt Dorothy's Tales* was published anonymously. She derived much amusement from hearing people talk about it, with many readers objecting to its melancholy ending. This first book was nevertheless reviewed favourably in the prestigious *Quarterly Review*, and in reading this she remained awake all night with joy. In 1839 her *Rambles in the South of Ireland* was a great commercial success, with the first edition selling out in a few weeks. She was a prolific writer of novels, tales, poems and travel accounts up until her old age. Among her travel books we should highlight the one published in 1841, *Home Sketches and Foreign Recollections*, an unexpected success even to her, and the two volumes of her unsuccessful *The Pyrenees with Excursions into Spain* (1843), a narrative of a long journey from Calais to the south of France and the Pyrenees including three short excursions into the Spanish regions of Catalonia and the Basque Country. She always travelled in the company of her husband, Lord Chatterton, whom she always refers to as W—, her maid (whose name is omitted throughout the whole narrative), and a little dog named Frisk, whose death near Bayonne during her six-month stay abroad was a truly sad event for her. While in France Lady Chatterton's narrative is centred on describing all the little villages and cities of their itinerary, for which she uses a whole arsenal of guidebooks whose abundant factual information she copies almost word for word. She takes special pleasure in describing her joy when she felt they had found good lodgings. Conscious of the difficulties of travelling for people like her, she stated that for an invalid,

> almost the entire pleasure of travelling depends upon the look of the rooms and the view from them, whether it be cheerful or otherwise; and therefore I think a little tour in those countries which have good inns, must be of great use to the spirits, if not to the health of sufferers. (vol. 3, pp. 16–17)

Lady Chatterton enjoyed her excursions to Spain more than any others in France. In Volume 3, chapter 10, she narrates their trip into Spain, visiting San Sebastian, the River Bidasoa and the towns of Irún and Hernani, whose beautiful scenery made a great impact on her. Even her first attempt at travelling by diligence proved more satisfactory than she had expected as she states: 'so far as our experience goes, it confirms what I have heard, that the diligence is the only comfortable way of travelling in Spain' (vol. 3, p. 207). Back at Pau Lady Chatterton enjoyed the company of the exiled Spaniards, who seemed to her very original and captivating (vol. 3, p. 303). In the Spaniards' houses, she observed, there were groups of pretty women, some at work, some sitting near the windows, looking out on the beautiful moon and the lovely views which it illuminated, standing out on the balcony, leaning over it in a truly Spanish attitude and holding their fans with the peculiar grace which belonged to that country of romance. The whole scene recalled to Lady Chatterton's mind the stories she had read and the pleasant dreams she had imagined of serenades and romantic lovers, of cruel parents and cross duennas. Then she emphasized that they had music too: *modinhas* and *boleros* sung by beautiful voices, and with that peculiar union of grace and force so striking in the national airs of Spain which strangers could seldom give. 'There is a sort of confiding affection shewn almost at first sight by most of the Spaniards I have seen', she says, 'which is very captivating and further removed from our English reserve than what we see in other foreigners' (vol. 3, p. 304). In chapter 18 she describes her excursions into Spain. She was transported in a *chaise à porteur*, carried by two men, with two to relieve them, plenty of provisions and a leather wine bottle to be used *à l'Espagnolle*. Their ride up the valley was delightful, as woods and mountains appeared in all their beauty. 'Here, in Catalonia', she continues,

> the Spanish women have a most sedate, and quite a regal air. You may fancy them born to be arch-duchesses and totally devoid of that frivolity which may be often seen in the French peasantry. They appear, too, far less amiable and desirous of pleasing, but to possess more solid goodness. They are very handsome, and have peculiarly fine lips and eyes, with clear and rather fair complexions and the most beautiful colour in their cheeks. (vol. 3, p. 392)

Chapter 20, the last of Volume 3, depicts their entrance into the Valley of Aran and their passing through numerous villages. The volume ends with Lady Chatterton's dismay at trying to prevent a few men from entering her room while she was in bed and attempting to convince the pretty daughter of the mayor of Viella of her objection to having a regular levee at her toilette. Then, after a while, with good humour the pretty young girl and her sedate companions slowly departed. Lady Chatterton felt an intense pleasure which was difficult to describe, she said, at getting safely back to France. After their long journey Lady Chatterton's health was delicate; she was too tired to eat or do anything, and she felt so ill that she thought that she was getting a bad fever. Lord Chatterton died in August 1855 and his widow married Edward Heneage Dering (b. 1827), who converted to Catholicism and presumably encouraged Lady Chatterton's conversion too in 1875, one year before her death.

Eroulla Demetriou

María Antonia López-Burgos del Barrio

José Ruiz Mas

Notes

1. Several meritable 'histories' of the genre of travel writing in the Peninsula in the last five centuries have been published during the twentieth century; the late eighteenth and early nineteenth centuries are the subjects of most of them. Some of these were addressed to an unspecialized readership or as introductory studies to the subject, such as I. Robertson, *Los curiosos impertinentes: viajeros ingleses por España 1760–1855* (Madrid: Editora Nacional, 1975, followed by several re-editions), D. Mitchell, *Here in Spain* (Fuengirola, Málaga: Lookout Publications, 1988) and P. Besas, *The Written Road to Spain. The Golden Decades of Travel: 1820–1850* (Madrid: Published by the author, 1988). For the specialized reader, we recommend the multi-authored *Imagen romántica de España,* 2 vols (Madrid: Ministerio de Cultura, 1981), B. Krauel Heredia, *Viajeros británicos en Andalucía de Christopher Hervey a Richard Ford (1760–1845)* (Universidad de Málaga, 1986), M. M. Serrano, *Viajes y viajeros por la España del siglo XIX* (Universitat de Barcelona, 1993) and most of M. A. López-Burgos del Barrio's work, which is focused mainly on nineteenth-century travel accounts on Spain. As regards American travellers in Spain throughout the nineteenth century, see P. Gifra-Adroher, *Between History and Romance: Travel Writing in Spain in the Early Nineteenth Century* (Chicago, IL: Associated Press, 2000) and A. Garrido Domínguez, *Viajeros americanos en la Andalucía del XIX* (Ronda, Málaga: Editorial La Serranía, 2007); regarding women travellers, see Garrido Domínguez, *Mujeres viajeras recorren la Andalucía del siglo XIX* (Ronda, Málaga: Editorial La Serranía, 2011). The latest international conference on travel literature on Spain was held at the University of Granada in 2005. It was attended by an academic elite of researchers and specialists on the genre and their contributions were published in *Viajeros británicos, irlandeses y norteamericanos en España: escritores, músicos y pintores/British, Irish and American Travellers in Spain: Writers, Painters and Musicians,* (eds) M. A. López-Burgos del Barrio and J. Ruiz Mas (Universidad de Granada, 2005).

2. For thorough bibliographical catalogues (and/or anthologies) of travel accounts on Spain and Portugal throughout the nineteenth century, see A. Farinelli, *Viajes por España y Portugal desde la edad media hasta el siglo XX: nuevas y antiguas divagaciones bibliográficas,* 4 vols (Roma: Accademia Nazionale dei Licei, 1979), J. García Mercadal's edition of *Viajes de extranjeros por España y Portugal,* 3 vols (Madrid: Aguilar, 1952–62; later re-edited in 2006 in 6 vols by the Junta de Castilla y León), R. Macaulay, *They Went to Portugal* (London: J. Cape, 1946), R. Foulché-Delbosc, *Bibliographie des voyages en Espagne et en Portugal* (Madrid: Julio Ollero Editor, 1991, which is a facsimile of the 1896 original work published in Paris: H. Welter), J. Alberich, *Bibliografía anglo-hispánica 1801–1850* (Oxford: The Dolphin Book Co., 1978), M. M. Serrano, *Las guías urbanas y los libros de viaje en la España del siglo XIX: Repertorio bibliográfico y análisis de*

la estructura y contenido (viajes de papel) (Universitat de Barcelona, 1993) and C. García-Romeral Pérez, *Bio-bibliografía de viajeros por España y Portugal (Siglo XIX)* (Madrid: Ollero & Ramos Editores, 1999).

3. For more information on this issue, see D. Saglia, *Poetic Castles in Spain: British Romantics and Figurations of Iberia* (Amsterdam: Rodopi, 2000), J. M. Almeida's edition of *Romanticism and the Anglo-Hispanic Imaginary* (Amsterdam: Rodopi, 2010) and J. Baptista de Sousa, *Almeida Garrett (1799–1854), Founder of Portuguese Romanticism: A Study in Anglo-Portuguese Cultural Interaction* (Edwin Mellen Press, 2011).

4. For more information, see J. Ruiz Mas's *Guardias civiles, bandoleros, gitanos, guerrilleros, contrabandistas, carabineros y turistas en la literatura inglesa contemporánea (1844–1994)* (Bern: Peter Lang, 2010).

5. Not much is known about Mrs Baillie's life. See Arthur Henry Grant's short biographical note of Mrs Baillie in the *DNB* (vol. 2, 1885).

6. For information on her life, see Twycross-Martin's entry about her in the *ODNB* (2004). The best primary source of information about her is *The Human Life and Letters of Mrs Ellis, Compiled by her Nieces* (London, 1893). For the understanding of the social context of Mrs Ellis's ideas and their impact, see L. Davidoff and C. Hall, *Family Fortunes: Men and Women of the English Middle Class, 1780–1850* (Suffolk: Routledge, 2002) and J. Flanders, *Inside the Victorian House: A Portrait of Domestic Life in Victorian England* (New York: W. W. Norton, 2004).

7. For information on Lady Chatterton's life, see George Clemens Boase's entry in the *DNB*, 1885–1900 (vol. 2) and *Memoirs of Georgiana, Lady Chatterton* (London: Hurst and Blackett, 1878), written by Edward Heneage Dering, her second husband.

CHRONOLOGY

c. 1795   Marianne Wathen is born.

c. 1810   (A few years before 1817) She marries Alexander Baillie.

1817   Mrs Marianne Baillie publishes *Guy of Warwick: A Legende. And Other Poems* (Kingbury: Printed by A.[lexander] Baillie), a very limited edition for her friends. In the preface she admits to being a 'novice' for having written poems 'of trifling value' and asks for benevolence to her art as she was 'laboring under the twofold disadvantage of sex and inexperience' (pp. vi, vii).

c. 1817   The Baillies go through 'hard times'.

1818   (Early months) The Baillies move to Twickenham under the protection of Baroness Howe (1762–1835), who was married to Sir Jonathan Wathen Waller (1769–1853), first Baronet and former oculist to King George III. Sir Wathen Waller was probably a distant relative of Marianne Baillie. In Twickenham the Baillies found 'shelter' and 'a calm relief'.

        (August–October) The Baillies set out on a tour to the Continent (France, Italy, Switzerland, Germany and Belgium).

1819   Mrs Baillie publishes *First Impressions on a Tour upon the Continent in the Summer of 1818, through Parts of France, Italy, Switzerland, the Borders of Germany, and a Part of French Flanders* (London: John Murray). She dedicates the book to Right. Hon. John Trevor (1748–1824, third Viscount Hampden), former British minister at Turin, 'a paternal friend'. The couple moves to Devonshire. Mrs Baillie writes 'Farewell to Twickenham', a poetical work.

1821   (June) The Baillies (who already have a young son) move to Portugal, as Mr Baillie is sent there to work on 'official duties' in Lisbon, presumably for the interests of the Earl of Chichester.

        (June–July) The Baillies settle in Lisbon. Marianne dislikes Lisbon and the Portuguese.

(July–October) She stays in the more agreeable town of Sintra. Her husband spends weeks on end in Lisbon. She feels lonely and homesick for England. She writes continually to her mother in England telling her about her life and her impressions of the country, the people, their customs, the political situation, the Portuguese royalty (João VI's family) and nobility, and so forth.

1821–3   (November 1821–October 1823) Resident in Lisbon. She gives birth to a daughter. She writes some poems which will be published in future poetical works and makes some excursions in the area. In the last few months of her Portuguese residence she becomes more positive about the Portuguese. The Baillies arrive in England in November 1823.

1824   Mrs Baillie publishes *Lisbon in the Years 1821, 1822, and 1823* (2 vols London: John Murray), consisting of sixty-five letters written to her mother, where she criticizes Portuguese bigotry, ignorance, narrow-mindedness, superstitions, papism, dirtiness, laziness, inefficiency, eating and dressing customs, education, and so forth. The travel account is dedicated to Thomas Pelham, second Earl of Chichester (1756–1826), a Whig politician and ex-Home Secretary under Henry Addington (1801–3) and the Joint Postmaster-General (1807–23) while the Baillies were in Portugal. Mr Baillie was working for him there, and they returned to England when the Earl of Chichester gave them leave to. They settle in London.

1825   Second edition of *Lisbon in the Years 1821, 1822, and 1823* (Edinburgh: J. Murray). Baillie also publishes *Trifles in Verse*, privately printed by her husband. Some of its poems had been written in Portugal.

1830   Mrs Baillie dies.

MARIANNE BAILLIE

Lisbon in the Years 1821, 1822, and 1823 by Marianne Baillie was originally published in two volumes in 1824 in London by John Murray in 12º, its price being 15s. It was re-edited one year later by J. Murray in Edinburgh in 1825 in 8vo. It includes sixty-five letters written to the author's mother while she was in Portugal. They are either signed with the initials M. B., or not signed at all.

Volume 1 consists of 219 pages (plus fourteen preliminary pages) and Volume 2 consists of 250 pages. Volume 1 includes letters 1 to 28, which is preceded by a dedication to the Earl of Chichester (p. 5) and a preface written by Baillie herself (pp. 7–16). Volume 2 includes letters 29 to 65.

The two volumes also include eight coloured pictures drawn by Mrs Baillie (published in June 1824, as is stated in every picture). The illustrations in Volume 1 are the following: 'Portuguese Lady Going to Mass' (p. 42), 'Portuguese Muleteer' (p. 55), 'Portuguese Peasants' (p. 90), 'Portuguese Scenery & Peasants' (p. 179) and 'Fisherman's Family of Pedroiços' (p. 237). The illustrations in Volume 2 are the following: 'Friars of Different Orders' (p. 105), 'Portuguese Nuns' (p. 171) and 'Portuguese Friars' (p. 201). The picture on the first page of both volumes depicting 'Belem Castle' was made by E. Finden, Sc.

In some of her letters Mrs Baillie also inserted a few poems (later to be made part of her *Trifles in Verse*, 1825). The poems in Volume 1 are 'Cintra' (pages 66–9, in letter 7) and 'The Exile's Lament' (pages 130–2, in letter 14). In Volume 2, the first is an untitled poem (its first line being 'Ah! Why is the moment thus given to joy', p. 102–3, in letter 38), 'Upon Seeing the Violet in the Garden of a Palace in Portugal' (p. 111–12, in letter 39) and another untitled poem (its first line being 'I wish I were in yon dear land', p. 214–16, in letter 56).

In the first volume, Mrs Baillie often omits the full names of many of the aristocrats, diplomats and military men alluded to, by simply giving an initial. In the second volume this practice is virtually dropped.

Several reviews exist of Mrs Baillie's travel account. These reviews are listed here in chronological order of publication:

— A review titled 'Lisbon' in the *Quarterly Review*,[1] by Robert Southey, who was the usual reviewer on Portuguese issues. He stated in his correspondence with John May on 16 March 1825 that he was writing a review at the time on Baillie's 'Lisbon'.

— An anonymous review titled 'Lisbon, in the years 1821–22–23' in *Blackwood's Edinburgh Magazine*.[2]

— An anonymous review in the *London Literary Gazette and Journal of Belles Lettres, Arts, Sciences*, where the book is described as 'full of feminine vivacity'.[4]

— An anonymous review in *The Modern Traveller. A Popular Description, Geographical, Historical, and Topographical, of the Various Countries of the Globe. Spain and Portugal*,[5] where we are informed of the price of the book (15*s*); and a repetition of the same review, this time signed by Josiah Conder, in the *Eclectic Review*.[6]

— An anonymous review in the *British Critic: New Series*.[7]

— An anonymous review in *Galignani's Magazine and Paris Monthly Review*.[8]

In *The World in Miniature. Spain and Portugal, Containing a Description on the Character, Manners, Customs, Dress, Diversions and Other Peculiarities of the Inhabitants of those Countries*, Frederic Shoberl repeats some fragments from Mrs Baillie's book word for word. He admits to having consulted Mrs Baillie's book (p. iv).[9]

In April 2002 Mrs Baillie's book was translated into Portuguese as *Lisboa nos anos de 1821, 1822 e 1823* by Albano Nogueira, who is also the author of its introduction.[10]

Notes

1. *Quarterly Review*, 31 (March 1825), pp. 378–90.
2. *Blackwood's Edinburgh Magazine*, 17 (April 1825), pp. 396–405.
3. *London Literary Gazette and Journal of Belles Lettres, Arts, Sciences* (1825), pp. 7–8.
4. Ibid, p. 7.
5. *The Modern Traveller. A Popular Description, Geographical, Historical, and Topographical, of the Various Countries of the Globe. Spain and Portugal*, vol 2 (London: James Duncan, 1826), p. 293.
6. *Eclectic Review*, 25 (January–June 1826), pp. 91–4.
7. *British Critic: New Series*; for January, February, March, April, May, June, 23 (1825), pp. 217–21.
8. *Galignani's Magazine and Paris Monthly Review*, 10 (1825), pp. 311–19.
9. *The World in Miniature. Spain and Portugal, Containing a Description on the Character, Manners, Customs, Dress, Diversions and Other Peculiarities of the Inhabitants of those Countries*. Illustrated with Twenty-Seven Coloured Engravings, 2 vols (London: R. Ackermann, 1827), p. iv.
10. A. Nogueira, *Lisboa nos anos de 1821, 1822 e 1823* (Lisbon: BN, 2002).

LISBON

IN THE YEARS 1821, 1822, AND 1823.

BY MARIANNE BAILLIE.

IN TWO VOLUMES.

VOL. I.

BELEM CASTLE.

LONDON:
JOHN MURRAY, ALBEMARLE-STREET.

MDCCCXXIV.

PREFACE. vii

far as circumstances may permit, into the
society of the natives; this has ever been
the wish of Mr. Baillie and myself, and we
therefore cultivated, as much as we could,
the acquaintance of the Portugueze; we
found them, generally speaking, by no means
social, or encouraging towards foreigners,
and I fear their usual character is not distinguished by frankness or urbanity. The
elegant author of " Recollections of the
Peninsula" accounts for this, somewhat at
the expense of the English; but although
there may be too much justice in what he
advances upon the subject, I cannot entirely
agree with him in the very favourable point
of view in which he describes Lisbon. With
him, every object is *couleur de rose;* his
glowing imagination reflects its own splendid
tints upon all he sees, and clothes really
disgusting realities in the brilliant garb of

viii   PREFACE.

enchantment.   Yet, am I fully persuaded,
that he wrote as he felt, and was unconscious of the delusion; nor am I surprized
at his feelings; he saw a southern country
for the first time, he was elevated by the
chivalrous spirit of his gallant profession,
and, more than all, was then at that blest
period of human existence,

" When all things please, for life itself is new."

To this may be added, that he probably
saw Lisbon at a more favourable moment
than the present; it was but just emanci-
pated from the dominion of the French police, which is known to have effected
miracles in the Augean task of freeing it from
its annoyances and impurities.   Mr. Matthews, in his "Diary of an Invalid," in
many respects fully corroborates the statements which will be found in the following

Letters. Whatever may be my general opinion in regard to the Portugueze, I should be guilty of a great omission, were I not to seize the opportunity of mentioning, with every sentiment of grateful esteem, the kindness we experienced from some families, who received us with the most genuine politeness and hospitality. To those of Anadia, Alva, Lacerda, and Torrebella, our acknowledgments are more particularly due; these individuals would grace the society of any country, and their merit is the more striking, from their having been born and educated in one which, it must be allowed, is somewhat behind the rest of Europe in civilization and refinement.

It so happened that during our residence there, (about two years and a half,) Portugal was agitated by different circumstances and

events, all of which were of the highest possible import, and calculated to awaken a
vivid degree of curiosity even in the mind
of the most apathetic observer.

To all who are interested in Portugueze
history (if their principles be those of justice
and liberality,) the conduct of the *constitutional* government during its brief reign must
appear almost incredibly base and imbecile;
never was opportunity so completely lost, or
power more shamefully abused. Had the
ministry been firm yet conciliating, rather
than overbearing, tyrannical and perfidious,
had they gradually introduced into their
councils the respectable portion of the nobility, sustained the true dignity of their
sovereign, and honoured religion in protecting the rights of the more virtuous part of
their clergy, and finally, had they enacted
a more moderate code of laws, it is probable
that they would have been encouraged and

assisted by other powers; but to every high minded principle they were utter strangers. These were trying times for the King of Portugal, as they would have been for a much wiser and more energetic monarch. His vacillation of conduct under late circumstances, should be viewed with indulgence, and his excuse may be found also in the general character of the nation; badly educated, they are still incapable of appreciating the blessings, or of using without abusing the rights of a free people; can it create wonder then, that they were found to be capricious and unstable? The King and people therefore are equally to be excused: he was naturally timid and complying, and they knew not precisely what to hope or to demand. It is much to His Majesty's credit, that, throughout, he has continued popular; he is humane and accessible,

b

an enemy to the dungeon and the scaffold, and these are indeed virtues in an absolute monarch.

A very amiable authoress, with whom I have much pleasure in being acquainted, has of late entered fully into the history of the defection of the Brazils from the mother country; it would be irrelevant to my subject, were I to touch upon the ground she has chosen, further than to corroborate the accuracy of her statements respecting that event. All good minds must hope that some satisfactory arrangement for both countries, will be ultimately effected; by which means any unnatural warfare between father and son may be prevented; some time nevertheless must be allowed, before the fermentation of spirits on either side, can reasonably be expected to subside; it is to be hoped too, that ere long, Portugal may open her eyes to the necessity of keeping on good terms with Great Britain, her ancient and best ally; should gratitude for past services, for the blood of its brave sons freely shed in her defence, cease to animate the mind of her rulers, let her look at the published list of her wine exports, even during the last two years, and self-interest alone would surely prompt her to remain steady to her friend; at all events, she will do well to reflect that *sudden* friendships are not always to be trusted.

The fate of some individuals for whom I cherish the most heartfelt esteem and regard, is so deeply involved in that of Portugal, that my wishes for the prosperity of the latter, will ever be as constant as they are sincere. I have found it necessary to curtail the relation of many circumstances, and wholly to omit others, the publication of which

xiv   PREFACE.

would very greatly heighten the interest of
these letters; the authoress to whom I have
already alluded, has expressed herself to
have been actuated by similar motives with
my own; and I most entirely coincide in her
sentiments where she observes, that " the
whole truth should not always be spoken."

LETTER II.

Buenos Ayres, June 30th, 1821.

YESTERDAY we set out in an open two-wheeled carriage (very like those old-fashioned vehicles to be seen in the prints of the earlier editions of Gil Blas), called a Sége, and drawn by a pair of small, long-tailed horses, of wretched appearance, one in the shafts, the other clumsily attached to his side, drawing only when ascending a hill, and bearing no share of the *weight*. The carriage itself was crazy, ill-contrived, and shabby in the highest degree, (but it was reckoned one of the best in Lisbon); and, thus accommodated, we proceeded to drive about the city, to view its principal squares, streets, &c. One of the largest of the former is the Terreiro de Páço, now called the Praça do Commercio. The equestrian statue in the centre, of Joseph I. is reckoned a work of merit. It is in bronze, of enormous proportions, and was modelled by Machado de Castro, a native artist. The Roscio is also a

8   LISBON.

large square, in which stands the Inquisition
(like the ancient lion in the fable), shorn of
its terrible teeth and claws. Let no one,
imagine, however, that either of these places
at all resembles Grosvenor or Portman
Square. At this time the former was filled
with loose and blinding sand, equally scorching to the eyes and to the feet, and neither
was adorned with a single shrub or blade of
grass. The people of Lisbon appear as if
they had even a greater antipathy to verdure
than Dr. Johnson, when he thundered forth
his contemptuous anathema against " green
fields" and those who " babbled of them."
Some few of the best streets, built since the
great earthquake, have flagged pavements;
among them are Gold Street and Silver
Street: the former chiefly inhabited by
jewellers, the latter by silversmiths. Haber-
dasher Street contains only tradesmen of
that description; and the silk-mercers, cloth-
merchants and linen-drapers have also their
streets appropriated generally to their different branches of trade, and called in like
manner after their professions. The shops
here are so inconveniently appointed that

the task of shopping becomes nearly impossible to females in the higher classes of society.

There are women who answer the description of female pedlars, who are frequently employed both by shopkeepers and ladies, and who run about the town retailing goods of various kinds, gaining a profit both from the purchaser and the tradesman. These very often unite the trade of smuggling to their other occupations, and are then called " Contrabandistas." I am told, that they abound both in this country and in Spain. The manufactories are still in a state of infancy, or of very inferior pretensions; they chiefly consist of silks, earthenware, snuff, and glass; but the importations from Germany have of late years more than rivalled the productions of the latter.

The only theatres are the Italian operahouse (San Carlos), and the Portugueze theatre; the former, which a few years since was remarkably rich in talent, is now so badly managed, as to be unworthy of any attention from foreigners; and the performers are so ill paid, as to have but little motive

10   LISBON.

for exertion. Of the latter I am not able to
speak, for I do not, as you know, understand
the language at present, and could therefore
be no judge of the merits of the actors.
We are assured, however, that, although
the style of the drama is of a very inferior
nature, there are several comic performers
here, who would do credit to any stage.
The streets, generally speaking, are not
well lighted, but still they are equal in this
respect to those of Paris, which is so ready
to claim a superiority over all the rest of the
civilized world!   At the door of every Ca-
sa·de Pasto, or public-house, we observed
the ancient symbol of a bush; but we are
assured that the wine found within is of so
excellent a quality, as to require no sign of
this nature.

We have tasted a sort of white light
wine, sold here, which we thought almost
as refreshing and as excellent as hock, and
for which the common charge is about two-
pence a bottle; it is made in the vicinity of
Lisbon, and is known by the name of vinho
de têrmo.   We remarked several equipages
in the streets—chiefly séges, but there were

some four-wheeled carriages also; both were equally shabby, clumsy, and inconvenient. The gentlemen in the inside were always without their hats, and the ladies many of them in full dress, with diamonds, although it was only noon! Of the principal public buildings, I cannot as yet pretend to give you any account, and I shall excuse my own indolence, and gratify your curiosity at once, by referring you to my future letters. The population is reckoned, I believe, at about 300,000 souls, and a fifth of the inhabitants are said to consist of negroes and mulattos; we observed some horrible specimens of the two latter! There are no circulating libraries to be found; the Portugueze have not hitherto patronized literature; which fact will not be disputed by any of our friends at home, when I tell them that there does not exist a good *Portugueze* edition of Camoens! almost the only native poet whose talent has risen at all above mediocrity! But where shall I find words strong enough to express the disgust of my feelings, when I reflect upon the appearance of the city in the aggregate, taking into ac-

count the personal appearance and customs
of some of its inhabitants! Here, every
sort of impurity appears to be collected together! You are suffocated by the steams
of fried fish, rancid oil, garlic, &c. at every
turn, mingled with the fœtid effluvia of decayed vegetables, stale provisions, and *other*
horrors, which it is impossible to mention—
to say nothing of the filthy dogs, of whom I
have formerly spoken. Wretches of a lower
and more squalid appearance than the most
sordid denizens of our St. Giles, lie basking
in the sun, near the heaps of impurity collected at the doors, while young women,
(and these of a more prepossessing personal
appearance, from whom one would naturally
expect greater delicacy in the olfactory
nerves,) hang far out of the windows above,
as if they were trying purposely to inhale
the pestilence which contaminates the air
beneath! Men and women, children and
pigs, dogs, cats, goats, diseased poultry,
and skeleton hogs, all mingle together in
loving fellowship, each equally enjoying
what seems to be their mutual element—
dirt! I must beg you to add to this, that

LISBON. 13

the armies of fleas, bugs, mosquitos, and
other vermin, are too numerous to be conceived even in idea, and the picture will be
complete! I am sorry to leave you at so
unfavourable a period of my description;
but I am obliged to conclude this letter in
haste. Adieu.

14   LISBON.

LETTER III.

SOCIETY, such as it exists in most other
great capitals of Europe, appears here to
be totally suspended or annihilated. During
the late peninsular war, and at a still more
remote epoch, we are assured that the utmost gaiety, variety, and sociality prevailed,
both among the numerous British residents
and ·some Portugueze families. *Now*, the
case is sadly changed. The English are
very few in number, and the native nobility,
clergy, and gentry, live in the most secluded
manner, showing little hospitality to foreigners, and maintaining but small intercourse with each other.   The unsettled
state of political affairs in some measure accounts for this.   Many of the best families
are either exiled by the new government,
upon suspicion of *ultra* sentiments, or are
still in attendance upon the Royal House of
Braganza, in Brazil.   The republican fac-

tion is small, but not perhaps the less dangerous upon that account. History abounds with examples of what has been effected by a handful of resolute and determined spirits. The Corcundas, or ultras, are held by the present faction in universal abhorrence, and the ascendency of a constitutional form of government seems to be very decidedly pronounced. The only Portugueze gentlemen to whom we have as yet been introduced, is Senhor F. de L——, the second son of the Baron do B——, and an officer in the army. His father now lies dangerously ill, which we are told has been the reason that the ladies of this family have not offered us those hospitable and polite attentions for which they have ever been justly celebrated, and which, in these times, have brought them into discredit with the most violent of the government party, who are inconceivably jealous of the English. Lisbon, indeed, has hitherto appeared to us, in every respect, to be " weary, stale, flat," and, I may truly add, " unprofitable;" for we have been assured by a most respectable merchant, who has long been settled here, that the comforts

16   LISBON.

indispensable to the establishments of English persons, are not to be obtained but at a greater expense than in our own country, with all its taxes.   In this opinion, our brief experience leads us perfectly to coincide. A bachelor, who ought in some measure to be a cosmopolite, may find a residence here, upon more advantageous terms; but a family man (unhappy wight!) will be lamentably disappointed and displeased.

The heat has now attained its utmost force.   Our window-shutters are closed to exclude the sun, and every door set open; but all is insufficient to relieve the oppression which the sudden change from a temperate to a hot climate has induced.   Yet the air, sultry beyond any I have ever yet felt, is thinner and more elastic than it is in England during an unusually hot summer.   We have not yet met with any good specimens of fruit; the cherries are generally very acrid, and strawberries extremely scarce; while the apricots, pears, plums, and oranges, (the latter being in season nearly the whole year,) are by no means finer than those we can purchase in England.

The same want of assiduous industry, which is so apparent in the culture of their vegetable and flower gardens, is equally visible in regard to the gifts of Pomona, who, to do her justice, has not here played the part of a step-mother. There are absolutely no such things in the city or its environs as either nursery grounds, flower shops, or gardeners regularly bred to the profession and living upon its rich and varied resources. If you desire a root of a rare carnation, or a cutting from any other particularly fine plant, you must either purchase from the gardener of some rich man, and thus give encouragement to dishonesty, or make up your mind to relinquish your wishes. —The chief *forte* of the Portugueze appears to lie in their ship-building and stone-masonry: several models of naval architecture are now proudly floating upon the Tagus; they have also some fine batteries, but are so ignorant of the art of managing these advantages, that, we are told by all *judges* upon the subject, the best of them would easily be silenced by an English frigate, in the space of half an hour. A

VOL. I. C

ship of fifty guns is at this moment stationed
here, for the purpose, it is *surmised*, of bringing off the British residents in case of any
extraordinary political commotion.   A packet from the Rio de Janeiro arrived last
night, with part of the king's suite on board;
but none of them have yet been allowed by
the new government to land, upon the *osten-
sible* pretext of their being unprovided with
passports.   Opinions vary respecting the
future conduct of this sovereign, who em-
barked (according to the intelligence brought
by the packet,) on the 26th of last April;
consequently, he may daily be expected in
the Tagus.   Don John VI., (or, as the Portugueze spell the name, Don João,) is rather
popular than not, and so indeed are the
whole house of Braganza.   If he accedes
with *a good grace* to the demands of the
Cortes, he may, and will be received with
applause by the great mass of the nation.
Among the upper classes, he has yet a considerable party, and the decided republicans
have *still appearances* to preserve, whatever
may be their interior feelings or ultimate
designs; therefore it is not very probable

that any great disorder or tumult will ensue upon his arrival: it is in an after period, comparatively distant, that scenes of agitation and fierce confusion may be more rationally expected.

The royal family consists of two sons and four daughters. The king's personal wealth and property are enormous; and no less than six men are said to have been employed at Rio, for the space of three successive days, in packing up his gold, previous to the embarkation: before the new order of affairs took place, he was in possession of *almost every thing* in Lisbon; but, at present, his income is considerably curtailed, so as to leave him at his disposal about £80,000 per annum. The revenues of the patriarch (the Pope of Portugal) were also incredible: he has been lately banished the country, on account of his refusal to take the constitutional oaths; but he has nevertheless recommended the clergy to do so. The church and convent of the Coracão do Jesus, usually called the Estrella, in the vicinity of Buenos Ayres, is one of the finest buildings of modern date; it was built by order of the late queen, and

at the expense of common sense, it might be
added, when it is remembered upon what
occasion, and in what an absurd spirit she
undertook its execution: she really imagined
herself to be in possession of the *heart* of
our Saviour, (a clear proof of her superficial
acquaintance with the most *important fact*
of Sacred History), which she enshrined in
a golden box, and in honour of which she
built this receptacle, calling it, as I have
already said, the church of the Coracão
(heart) do Jesus. The Pope was unwilling
at first to comply with her request of found-
ing a new order of nuns upon the occasion;
but afterwards yielded his better judgment
to her importunities; thus preferring to
bring contemptuous ridicule upon sacred
subjects, rather than disappoint the wishes
of an earthly sovereign. The building in
question, though of far smaller proportions,
is upon much the same plan as our St. Paul's,
and is constructed wholly of a sort of bastard
marble; near to it are the hospital, church,
and burial ground of the English factory,
established many years since by Mr. de
Visme: the former is an excellent institu-

LISBON. **21**

tion, and the latter by far the most shady
and the prettiest spot in the neighbourhood:
it contains many a melancholy memorial of
grief and tenderness; and the pale demon
of consumption may here plume her spectral
wings, and grin a ghastly smile of compla-
cence upon counting the number of her victims.   Adieu.

LETTER IV.

Buenos Ayres, July, 1821.

AT length, we are fairly driven away from Lisbon by the tremendous heat of the weather! nothing but a native or a sala-mander can exist here, at this season! Cin-tra is to be our retreat, where we are encou-raged to hope for temperate and refreshing breezes, and all the welcome luxury of shade. This step is as necessary as it is agreeable, for my strength has completely given way, under the influence of varied ailments, pecu-liar to *newcomers!* My child is scarcely recognizable, from the incessant stings of the mosquitos, in every part of his body, nor am I in a much better condition; a per-petual succession of restless and feverish nights, occasioned by the persecution of these horrid insects, is no longer endurable! —I agree with Mr. Matthews in his " Diary," that " there is almost always a hot sun and a cold wind with it, in Lisbon ;" had we given due credit to this author's friendly cautions, had we allowed more to the sensible and accurate observer, and thought less of the fastidious *Invalid*, while perusing his journal, we should not perhaps have quitted the known comforts of our own country for the uncertain pleasures of this land of the Sun! I formerly used to fancy every thing connected with *winter*, cheerless and undesirable, and was fully persuaded that I should enjoy with delight a perpetual summer: *now* when experience forces me to open my eyes to the *truth*, I am but too well convinced of the benefit and charm of a change of seasons, such as we are accustomed to see at home; and while I cast my dazzled eyes, upon the intolerable glare of blue sky and water, heightened by barren rocks, and faint beneath the scorching beams of the sun, " shining in his strength," I remember with a sigh the cheerful hearth, the close drawn curtain, and the music of the kettle, " singing on the hob," which I used to enjoy during the winter in our English cottage residence! *Cowslip* exclaims, " Talk of Venus and her doves! give me a roast duck!" and in a

similar spirit, could I now say, " Talk of
vineyards and of fountains! give me a good
fireside!" How perverse is the human heart,
or rather, how deceitfully flattering are the
promises of Imagination! I think I may be
the better probably, during the rest of my
life, for the lessons a sojourn in Portugal
have afforded me—the bee draws honey
from the bitterest plants!

This evening I have amused myself by
trying to sketch from my window a group
of street musicians, the raggedest sons of
Apollo I ever saw!—two men and a boy,
filthy wretches all! monotonously thrum-
ming upon a couple of cracked guitars, a
doleful accompaniment to their hoarse and
wiry voices! The costume of the lower
orders would not be unbecoming, if they
had a more thorough notion of personal
cleanliness; when they walk out, it invariably consists, (in summer or in winter,) of a
long ample cloth cloak, generally of a brown,
black, or scarlet colour, with a deep falling-
cape, called a " capote," which forms a
graceful drapery, both to men and women;
the latter wear a white muslin handkerchief

Drawn by M.Baillie.

PORTUGUEZE LADY GOING TO MASS.

Published June, 1824, by John Murray, London.

doubled cornerways, carelessly thrown over
their dark braided locks, and fastened beneath the chin: when they go to mass, on
festivals or Sundays, they carry a fan in the
hand, and frequently assume an air of gravity
and importance, bordering upon the super-
cilious; this, however, exists chiefly among
the *old* women; the younger ones have a
gay cheerful expression of countenance, and
quick glancing eyes as brilliant and as dark
as jet; *all* wear pink, green, or yellow silk
shoes, or even white satin, and worked
stockings, (the latter knitted very ingeniously
by the peasants,) even in the midst of the
most disgusting dirt and mud; the trade of
shoemaker must be a profitable one in this
country! The class one step higher in the
scale of society indulge in tawdry ill-chosen
finery, in *sorry* imitation of the French and
English fashions; but at mass, they exchange
this gaudy attire for a black silk gown, and
a deep transparent veil, of the same sombre
hue, which latter they throw over their heads
without any other covering, even in the coldest
day of winter: their *religion* induces this
chastity of taste in decoration, and I wish it

26   LISBON.

produced an equally beneficial result in other
respects! Some few youthful faces which
I have seen, appear pretty enough; the
great charm being produced by the dark
and brilliant eye, and depth of eyelash, to
which I have already alluded; and although
the complexion is *generally* sallow, and almost without exception, brown, I have once
or twice remarked a very rich and beautiful
glow, like the bloom of a crimson carnation,
upon the cheek. The *old* women appear to
me, from the specimens I have hitherto seen,
to be *invariably* hideous; we are given to
understand, that the higher the rank of the
people in this country, the plainer in feature
they generally become, and that with some
few exceptions, it is among the peasantry
alone, that true beauty exists. I have not
yet dared to glance at the customs of a
Portugueze kitchen, for the *accounts* I receive are really too alarming, to be closely
investigated: we have arrived at this hotel,
(kept by very obliging English people,)
in rather an unlucky hour, as they have
parted with their cook, and are not yet provided with her successor, and the cookery

calling itself English, is just now detestable
in consequence.   The meat sold here is
disgustingly prepared, owing to the ignorant
method of the Portugueze butchers in killing
it.   Veal, in the environs of Lisbon, is prohibited by the laws, and all that comes to
table is smuggled: this regulation, I rather
think, was instituted with a view of preserv-
ing the breed of cattle, for the purposes of
the dairy and the yoke; cows being in high
request, (as goat's milk is the more common
resource here,) and oxen are used for drawing carts and waggons: the breed of horses
is small and delicate, consequently wholly
unfit for heavy burthens or draught: the
cows are unhappy animals; for there is little
pasturage at *any* season, and *now* they are
fed upon turnips, cabbages, &c. &c., which
renders their milk poor, and of an impure
flavour.   Butter is *imported* from Ireland
and England; of course it is all salted, and
in summer becomes very rancid and oily:
potatoes are grown here, but in such small
quantities that they are imported likewise
from the same places.   An epicure would
certainly commit suicide were he condemned

28 LISBON.

to pass a month in Lisbon, unless he happened to be exclusively fond of fish, which
abound in the Tagus, and of various sorts
and superior excellence: John Dorys and
Turbot, the dear-bought solace of many an
aldermanic soul, are here as cheap as her-
rings in England, and are looked upon with
contempt, as an inferior food.

I am really so much indisposed with the
various accumulated annoyances which we
meet with at every turn, heightened by the
aggravation of intense hot weather, that I
can write no longer: if I were to attempt a
continuation, this letter would resemble an
apothecary's memorandum book—such a list
of pains and aches! in mercy to *you*, therefore, as well as to myself, I will say adieu.

LETTER V.

Buenos Ayres, July.

I AM quite in spirits at the idea of our speedy removal to Cintra, Dr. W. our English physician, having declared it absolutely necessary for my health and that of the child—in return for his agreeable advice, I am ready to pronounce him " a second Daniel!" This gentleman enjoys a high reputation both for medical talent and for private worth; and he is so kind to the poor, that they have universally named him, " *Santo* W***." We do not hear a very encouraging account of the learned faculty in this country; with some honourable exceptions, they seem to have made little progress since the days of Doctor Sangrado, of deathless memory, and his plan, which in the time of Gil Blas was so much approved in Spain, is *now* quite the fashion *here:* but we must not be too severe in our reprobation of foreign practitioners, when we allow so

much credit to mere *theory* in the art, even
in the bosom of our own enlightened metropolis!

Early this morning, we were saluted by
the intelligence of the King's having entered
the Tagus, and being in full sail up the river.
The Cortes have sent to inform his Majesty
that he *cannot be permitted* to land until to-
morrow, nor indeed *at all,* unless he confirms and sanctions the late proceedings of
that body: had this event been predicted
to him when he first mounted the throne, it
would doubtless have been considered as
idle as the warnings of Cassandra: and
yet the spirit of the age, so universally hostile to a *despotic* form of government, might,
to a discerning monarch, have been clearly
perceptible years ago.!   The King is come
over in a line-of-battle ship, originally built
at Lisbon, and named after himself, " Don
João Sesto;" it has now anchored so near
us, that we can discern with our tele-
scopes what passes on board; she is surrounded by small boats, crowded with
people, among whom we plainly distinguish

the King's rowers, dressed in scarlet, with gilt plates on the front of their caps: the river, and its far distant shores, resound with the roar of various royal salutes, poured from the brazen throats of every gun on board the numerous ships of all nations now in the harbour: the English frigate, the Liffey, Captain Duncan, is covered with innumerable flags of the gayest variety of colour, and the crew are attired in their gala costume; they are swarming amid the rigging, as well as upon deck, like clustering bees, and I can perceive some of the officers fearlessly stationed at the same dizzy height! Two Russian ships, besides this frigate, are now riding at anchor here—it is impossible, therefore, that the King should entertain much fear as to his personal safety, while he remains under the observation of such powerful defenders: his best security, however, will be the affection and confidence of his people—the King who has once taken possession of the *heart* of his subjects, needs not any other rampart than their arm; he may defy foreign enmity, and dispense with foreign protectors ! — nevertheless, I cannot but commiserate the unpleasant sensations which must certainly at this moment oppress the mind of Don João, especially as he himself is said to be painfully aware of his own incapacity.

(10 *o'clock at night.*) The popular mind is certainly in favour of the King; every creature who can command the use of a lamp, has hung out this token of his joy: the palace of the Ajuda, and the houses of the upper and middle classes, are lighted from the ground floors to the garrets; but any *real* splendour or taste in this species of decoration, is no where to be seen: the Portugueze do not seem to have the slightest idea of any superior method of illumination, than plain shabby little lamps, resembling lanthorns.—I must break off my letter, which I will conclude to-morrow.

(*Wednesday, July 4th.*) Mr. B. went early to Lisbon this morning, to witness the landing of the King, who has complied with every demand of the New Government;

his first act was to repair at the head of a grand procession to the Madelena Church, to offer up thanks upon his safe arrival: his countenance had a wild and distrustful expression, and he appeared to go through the different parts of the ceremony with mechanical formality; he may really be pardoned for seeming a little bewildered; poor man! he was probably tempted more than once to doubt his own identity! Count Palmella (late ambassador to our court) is among the number of persons suspected and disliked by the present government: some of the royal followers are arrested as state prisoners, and the Count, they say, will be banished from Lisbon. The general opinion seems to be, that the King will make no attempts at resistance for the present, *if ever*; and that he, in fact, could not act otherwise, even if he had the inclination, as the Constitutionalists have so completely the reins in their hands, that any opposition on his part would be an act of insanity.

This is certainly a very interesting political moment, even to the most indifferent observer; for it is almost impossible not to be of

84   **LISBON.**

opinion, that the revolutions now effected in
Spain and Portugal will be followed, sooner
or later, by similar and still more eventful
changes upon the rest of the continent—I
might perhaps say, of the *world!*   Adieu.

LETTER VI.

Cintra.—Costa's Hotel, July.

HERE we are at Cintra! but in order
that you may *fully* enter into the delightful
change of situation and of feeling which we
now enjoy, I must carry you once more
back to the last morning of our sejour at
Buenos Ayres: what would the bright
lights of Rembrandt be worth, if deprived
of the contrast of their shades? After a
sleepless night then, during which the perpetual howling of the dogs in the street,
and the dull clang of the bells belonging to
innumerable convents or churches, had rendered me more than usually irritable, I beheld with joy the first dawn of the day
which was to witness our removal; when
the sun arose, I had a strong inclination to
get up to admire so magnificent a spectacle;
but I was checked by indisposition and indolence, and also sadly recollected, that this
bright luminary could *here* shed his flood
of glory upon barren rocks and water only!

D 2

36   CINTRA.

Here was no " pomp of groves or garniture of fields," to yield glad incense in return for his smile: dear England! how thy purity, cleanliness, freshness and comfort, rose in painful intensity before me! what a contrast to the actual scene did thy verdant meadows, thy superb oak woods, and thy cool, sedge-crowned rivers then present!—but enough of this.

We now ascended the sége, and were forthwith bolted up, together with sundry boxes and baskets, whose sharp edges every moment pressed painfully against our knees, and which, by the time that we had gone five miles, completely rubbed the skin off our shins :* I must here record, by way of episode, that our heavier leather trunks were sent under the charge of an almocrêve, or carrier, in a rude sort of cart, drawn by oxen, the wheels of which, made of solid blocks of wood, creak and groan (as if in despair at the burthen they carry) in the most discordant and lamentable manner; the

---

* There is no accommodation for luggage, in these most inconvenient carriages.

Drawn by M. Baillie.

PORTUGUEZE MULETEER.

Published June 1824, by John Murray, London.

drivers would not grease them upon any account, " for the *noise* (they say) keeps off the evil spirits from men and beasts:" our trunks, however, upon arriving at Cintra, had been treated most *diabolically*, for their neat appearance was completely spoiled, they were rubbed into holes, and their contents scarcely saved from consequent injury: a little straw would have obviated this, but the Lusitanian sages (being, I suppose, of the school of Diogenes) never trouble their heads about such frivolous niceties of refinement. Off we drove, descending the steep, roughly paved streets of Buenos Ayres, clattering, jangling, shattering, and jolting along, conducted by a gaunt swarthy postilion, in " a loose chamois doublet" and rusty hat; we left the hotel at seven o'clock, and were more than four hours in reaching Cintra, a distance of fifteen miles: the road is rudely paved the whole way, nor is there, as in France, the resource of the narrow " *terre*'. by the side of the "*pavé;*" and, even at this early hour, the heat was extremely oppressive: we were accompanied by a friend, who acted as our interpreter on the road, who was

mounted upon a favourite Spanish horse, of
rather small proportions, yet extremely handsome: the head quite a model for the sculptor; but the horses of this country are distinguished by a want of roundness in the hind
quarter, a narrowness in the contour of the
hip, which I am sure Praxitiles would never
have pardoned, either in a barb or a beauty.
We stopped to refresh the animals, at a casa
de pasto (public house), about half way between Lisbon and Cintra; the group of
figures collected in the dark miserable
kitchen, was very striking to an *inexperi-
enced* eye; our host, a round visaged, quick-
eyed, greasy wight, bustled out to receive
us, as nimbly as his rotundity of form would
allow; he was a true specimen of what Cervantes calls " a rascally don peasant, stuffed
with garlic," and might have passed for the
twin brother of my dear old friend Sancho
Panza.*   The costume of this worthy may
be described in few words; upon his back
he had a skirtless *something,* which once

---

* He, I afterwards discovered, was always designated
" Sancho."

had been a jacket; and his loose mud-coloured nether garments were stuffed into a pair of boots, which looked as if they were used as candle-boxes, when not wanted by the wearer; behind him, stood two or three women, among whom was his daughter, considered the belle of the place: she was certainly a very handsome brunette, with a spot like the pomegranate blossom in each of her plump cheeks, and many a senhora of high degree might have envied her the eyes and smile; but the disgusting negligence and dirt of her attire and person, completely destroyed the effect of her beauty. One other member of this company was not the least remarkable among them; a woman in the last stage of lean and withered old age; I believe I have already told you, that advanced life among the lower class of females, *here* seems to assume a ten-fold ghastliness of appearance: this animated mummy stood leaning upon a staff, her sunken eyes fixed on vacancy, and her lips moving without any audible sound, as she slowly counted the beads of an immense black rosary, which hung from her trembling tan-coloured hand:

40   CINTRA.

upon receiving a trifle, she slightly recovered
her recollection, and nodding her Sibyl head,
(whose thin grey locks were braided as in
the days of her youth, and devoid of any
other covering than the ordinary handkerchief, which had fallen back,) made the sign
of the cross upon her skeleton breast! The
inn itself, if inn it could be called, was so
dirty and sordid in its outward appearance,
that I should as soon have attempted entering the kraal of a Hottentot; and I could
certainly have borne many a keen pang of
hunger, before I brought myself to taste any
viands it might contain, the chief of which
would, we were told, invariably consist of
coarse salt fish, rancid oil, and garlic. We
now proceeded on our route, and at length,
after having traversed a barren sandy monotonous tract of country, for the greater part
of the way, we began to perceive a slight
change for the better; the atmosphere became less oppressively hot, and here and
there a few trees refreshed our wearied
eyes, while a grand looking mountain, its
highest and most fantastic peak, crowned

by a picturesque Convent, rose in proud magnificence before us. A handsome quinta (i. e. country house,) gave an air of refinement to the nearer scene; its white walls starting forward, in full relief, from a back ground of dark green foliage, formed an agreeable picture; but this verdant retreat appeared nevertheless to stand alone, in the midst of a still bald and arid country, like an emerald set in copper!—The landscape now gradually increased in interest; an ancient mansion belonging to the queen, called Ramalão, appeared on the left, which was by no means devoid of beauty, though somewhat of a quaint and formal order; shortly afterwards we turned suddenly round a corner of the mountain, and then Cintra, that beautiful paradise, burst upon our sight, in all its matchless loveliness and grandeur! How shall I describe this fair, this exquisite spot of earth? my weak powers shrink from the attempt! let me endeavour to give you some idea of the view which greeted my eyes, from the windows of my bed-room, upon awakening early the morning after our

42   **CINTRA.**

arrival; but this, upon second thoughts, is too much for the *end* of a letter: I will give it you in my next.

———

LETTER VII.

Cintra, July.

You are to fancy me (as I told you in my
last) seated at the window of my apartment,
in the hotel at Cintra; the room itself
was not devoid of charm to my peculiar feelings, a charm which would not strike every
other person, as it arose wholly from *association*; its whitewashed walls, clean boarded
floor, and simple old fashioned wooden chairs,
reminded me of some which I remembered to have seen in respectable English
farmhouses, deep in the bosom of the country, far removed from the luxury and pretension to refinement, which distinguish
similar dwellings nearer the *metropolis :* the
snowy white dimity bed, and *prim* little toilette table, covered with coarse frilled muslin,
delightfully clean, gave an idea of purity,
order, and comfort, which was truly refreshing both to the body and to the spirits;
particularly when contrasted with the dirt
and closeness of most continental sleeping

44   CINTRA.

rooms: but let me open the window, (about
which I have kept your imagination so long
hovering,) and thus admitting the fresh
morning breeze, lose all recollection of past
annoyances, in the crowd of agreeable sensations which now throng upon each other.
What a gale of fragrance rises from beneath,
from all around! the orange and lemon
trees, which here grow to an enormous size,
in the rich garden, or rather orchard, below,
fling their mingled perfume (from fruit and
blossom) to the soft wind, which blows from
the ocean, whose blue waters I can distinctly
perceive (at a distance of about six miles)
sparkling in the sun; yet it does not appear more than two miles from me, such is
the extraordinary clearness of the atmosphere; the scent of lavender and rosemary
mix with that of the spicy carnation, which
flourishes in antique-shaped earthen pots,
or in deep layers of earth, upon the top of
the stone walled garden of every quinta.   I
view beneath the nearer mountains, an universal profusion of fruit trees, at whose feet,
the wood-strawberry blushes behind her
delicate leaves: in the garden of this hotel,

the Alpine sort is cultivated, as well as the
white and red raspberry; both fruits are
considered in Portugal as luxuries; here
and there, I can perceive a small patch of
ground, hung high among the surrounding
crags of rock, where, carefully shaded from
the sun, by hedges of palm, and sedulously
watered from the numerous stone cisterns, or
fountains, with which every quinta abounds,
the lettuce and other vegetables, requiring
a cooler climate, are cultivated: a confused
yet soothing murmur of falling waters, of
wild bees, and of birds, warbling *almost* as
sweetly as those in England, (among which
the note of the ringdove is pre-eminent,)
delights the ear, while a cloudless heaven of
summer blue, sheds light, and life, and joy,
upon every object! Nothing surely can be
more enchanting than such a prospect; and
yet a walk of ten minutes from the hotel,
will afford the lover of the sublime a still
more perfect landscape. I allude to the
grounds of the Marialva Palace, or to those
of the Pénha Verde Quinta, from whence
the superb addition of towering mountain-
scenery may be enjoyed. I find, however,

46   CINTRA.

that *plain prose* will not suffice, to give any
adequate idea of this; take therefore a little
effusion in verse, in which I could not refuse myself the *relief* of indulging, upon the
second morning of our arrival.

CINTRA.

Dull sleep, begone! I spurn thy poppied crown,
Thy spell Circean, potent though it be;
Hence! seek thy votaries in yon sickly town;
These scenes of life, these breezes pure and free,
Thou nodding Sibyl, were not made for thee!

The glorious sun is ris'n! o'er Cintra's dale,
(Fairer methinks than poet's haunted dream,)
He smiles in light, and rends the misty veil
From yonder mountain's brow, whence many a stream,
Dancing in joy, springs forth to catch his beam!

Swift let me climb the crag's romantic height,
And gain the shelter of yon hermit seat;
A bower of bliss, befitting lady bright,
For stern ascetic all too wildly sweet;
Here let me gaze around, and rest my pilgrim feet.

Far overhead, piercing the vaulted sky,
The convent of " Our Lady of the Rock,"*
In calm pre-eminence of majesty,
Rears its grey walls, braving the tempest's shock,
And at the earthquake's terrors seems to mock!

                    * Nossa Senhora da Pénha.

CINTRA.   47

Yet the convulsions of a changing state,
The storms of *human* ire, may lay thee low !
Perchance at thee, 'ere long, may stern-eyed fate,
Launch her red lightnings, aim the whelming blow,
And give thine humbled sons a deep reverse to know.

Look out, grey Padres ! view the wreck of power,
Mark well the lesson taught by yonder pile;
The mouldering remnant of the Moorish Tower,*
The turban'd Infidel's strong hold, 'ere while,
When on this prostrate land, he glanced his victor
            smile !

From monuments of human pride and woe,
Gladly I turn, pure Nature's charms to greet;
Heaven ! what a joyous prospect laughs below !
What golden orchards, gardens fair and sweet,
And waving woods, in bright confusion meet !

Where leafy groves in mingled foliage gleam,
The cork-trees spread on high their rugged arms;
The hoary fathers of the wood they seem,
Protecting the acacia's bending charms,
The trembling ash, and youthful beech from harms !

The walnut there, expands her verdant screen,
Near her, the chestnut rears her graceful head ;
The pensive cypress darkly waves between,
And lofty fir, on mountain summit bred,
Looks down on the pomegranate blushing red !

          * O Castello dos Mouros.

48   CINTRA.

Hark to the varied sounds which gradual swell,
Borne on the breeze, they soothe the listening ear;
The ring-dove murmuring in the lonely dell,
The gush of many a fountain, cold and clear,
And bell of climbing goat, or roving muleteer:

While nearer still, the wild-bee's fairy horn
Continual rings around my green retreat,
As from the dewy cups, at early morn,
Of every mountain flower, th' aroma sweet,
She ceaseless culls, to form her winter treat.

List to the sun-bright ocean's distant sound!
Yonder its dark blue waters gently lave
The pebbled shore, which fertile plains surround;
Their yellow harvests undulating wave,
And call the reaper's care, their golden stores to save.

Hard by, the olive and the purple vine,
Their mingled treasures lavishly bestow;
Oh favour'd land! thus corn, and oil, and wine,
Along thy happy vallies ever flow,
And bid man's ravished heart, in grateful warmth to
          glow!

What blended fragrance loads the passing gale!
The balmy breath of many an herb and flower;
Incense delicious, rising from the vale,
Where orange groves their fruits and blossoms shower,
And rich carnations bloom in jasmine bower.

CINTRA. **49**

Thus do the sights, the sounds, the scents of bliss,
Combine to charm! O earth! how fair thou art!
Had fabled Arcady a vale like this?
Could scenes of Eden deeper touch the heart,
Or through the sense a keener rapture dart?

O work sublime! here best I trace the hand,
Th' almighty hand, which formed the glorious whole;
Can ransomed man with frozen bosom stand,
Nor own thy love, nor bless thy mild controul?

Eternal Saviour! humbly thus I bend!
With prostrate heart, in adoration bow:
How my 'rapt thoughts on eagle wings ascend
To thy bright throne, where seraphs veil the brow!
Teach me to praise thee! Father, teach me how!

I dare say some of the thoughts, or rather the expressions in these lines, may not be wholly original; the memory is frequently treacherous upon these occasions, leading us to forget that we have drawn our images from *her sources*, rather than from those of invention; but be this as it may, I wrote the above, almost without a pause, yet found them at the conclusion, quite inadequate to express that mingled rapture of admiration and delight, which filled my mind upon first beholding the scenes to which they allude.

50   CINTRA.

LETTER VIII.

Cintra, July.

EVERY body who arrives here from Lisbon is of course eagerly questioned as to the state of political affairs.   The accounts never vary in respect to the quiet and resigned *submission,* if I may so call it, of the King. He has fixed his residence at the palace of Queluz, which he has ever preferred to that of the Ajuda, on account of its superior gardens.   A lady who called upon me this morning, and who has passed twenty years of her life in this country, related an anecdote of the King upon his first arrival at Queluz, strikingly characteristic of that tenaciousness of etiquette, which sufficiently evinces the *real* state of his feelings, however he may continue to repress their more serious ebullition.   Entering one of the state apartments, he observed chairs placed

* *Queluz*—This, literally translated, means "what a light !"

there, which is an unusual circumstance;
" what is all this, what is all this?" said he,
" how came these chairs here?" To which
the attendants replying that they were intended for the use of the Cortes, when they
came to pay their duty to his Majesty, he
quickly rejoined, " The Cortes! take them
away instantly! no person shall ever use a
chair in my presence!"—All the Royal Family have hitherto been approached on the
knee only; and a Portugueze lady and her
daughters, in rather delicate health, com-
plained to me very lately, that it was always
so great a fatigue to them to pay a visit to
the Queen and Princesses in their own
apartments, that they usually went to bed
immediately after their return from the royal
presence, and this in consequence of their
being obliged to remain kneeling the whole
time that these high personages chose to
prolong the conversation! When they go
abroad, every body, no matter how illustrious their rank, (for the first nobility are
looked upon by the King as *his servants*,)
are under the necessity of descending from
their carriages or horses, and of humbly

saluting them as they pass, to which they seldom return even the slightest inclination of
the head; this is an abuse of prerogative,
which if it should be henceforward abolished, will not, *cannot* be regretted by the
most loyal and attached friends of the monarchy : but how *much* is there still existent
which needs reform in every department of
the government !

I am as yet ignorant of the existing character of the Portugueze clergy, generally
considered ; but the following anecdote relative to an individual *padre*, which was related to me by an English gentleman, does
not greatly prepossess a protestant in its
favour. " A woman in the lower class of society, being oppressed by the weight of some
family misfortune, went to one of the
churches to pray; she was found by this
priest upon her knees, pouring out her sup-
plications to that Almighty Redeemer, who
alone is able to save ! " Why do you pray
to Jesus Christ ?" said he : " apply rather to
such and such *saints*, for they are so powerful in heaven, that they are able to do every
thing for you, and may ask *whatever they*

choose of Jesus Christ, *who dares not refuse them!"* I cannot, however, bring myself to believe this tale! The common people at Lisbon are all much *horrified* at the idea of *our* priests being allowed to marry; the former minister of the English factory resident there, had for a length of time continued to be greatly respected among them, until they heard that he was upon the point of returning to England, with an intention of being married; then indeed he sunk at once in their estimation, nor were all his virtues able to save his memory from reproach and scandal. Our present clergyman came hither accompanied by his wife, and, for the first few months after her arrival, she could not appear in the streets without being pointed and gazed at, with displeased curiosity by the populace, as " the *English padre's wife.*"

Cintra has been illuminated in honour of the King; the effect of the lights sparkling in the windows of the different quintas, perched high among the mountains, embosomed in dark woods, was singularly beautiful!—beheld by moonlight it is in-

deed a scene of fairy land! such a superb
moon I have hardly ever seen as that which
at this time looks down upon us! I wonder
not at the ancient worship of that " queen
of heaven," and this reminds me of it's
having been formerly called by the Romans,
" the promontory of the moon," the name of
Cintra being a corruption of " Cynthia," and
the remains of a small temple dedicated to
this goddess have been discovered upon the
summit of the highest mountain in the
neighbourhood. I can never forget the impression which this charming scenery made
upon my imagination, when I contemplated
it for the first time by this light; the
white-walled quintas, rising amid the deep
woods I have already mentioned, (whose
waving foliage then appeared *black* as the
plumes of the gigantic helmet of Otranto,)
assumed a pale ghostly effect, which was
infinitely striking: the shaded lanes were
full of glow-worms, and the fire-flys darted
from bough to bough; these last are very
lovely delicate insects; the phosphoric matter is confined to the lower part of their
slender bodies, and is of a more *rubied* lustre

than that of the glow-worms, which appear
to me like living emeralds.

I have been standing every night in the
open gallery which runs on the outside of
the hotel, and communicates with the sitting
rooms, somewhat in the style of the Swiss
farm-houses, enjoying the balmy and refreshing air: but I am warned against this
practice, however delightful to the feelings,
as the neighbourhood of the mountains induces a very heavy fall of dew and vapour
at the decline of day. I ought to mention
one sublunary circumstance, to which I am
shocked at perceiving I am by no means so
indifferent as so romantic an admirer of *un-
sophisticated* nature ought to be! I allude
to the excellent fare which we meet with
at this hotel. Good butter, daily fresh from
the churn, (Cintra being the only place so
near Lisbon where such a luxury is to be
procured,) fruits glowing from their parent
trees, good cow's milk, and water the purest
that ever gushed from its crystal source in
the hidden recesses of the mountains, to say
nothing of the Vinho do Colares, a delicate

56   CINTRA.

claret-flavoured wine, made at a village of
that name, very near this place. The talents
of an excellent French cook add to all these
comforts not a little.   Adieu.

———

LETTER IX.

Cintra, July.

I CANNOT tell you how much I lament the necessity which has called away Mr. B. from this delightful retreat, and which plunges him once more into Lisbon's fiery furnace! We are, certainly, at a most inconvenient distance from the latter place, and nothing but *health* induces me to remain in a situation which thus divides our establishment, and leaves me so much and so frequently alone, surrounded by strange faces, and obliged, during his absence, to live almost entirely in my own apartments, to avoid the stare of rude curiosity.—This evening we have been riding out upon burinhos, or burricos (*i. e.* donkeys), which are in universal request at Cintra; they are strong handsome animals, very different (generally speaking) from the smaller sized ragged and stupid asses, common to England; some of them are full of spirit, with regular paces, and are as sleek and well curried as horses; nor is it at all unusual to give ten moidores* a piece for them; we set off at six o'clock, just as the heat of the day was over, accompanied by a friend, carrying the child before him upon his burinho—a dark-eyed sallow boy, and a mongrel cur (the inseparable friend of the latter) were our only attendants. We rode through a rocky defile, overhung with cork trees, than which nothing but our own match-less oaks can be grander; at every step some new beauty in the landscape arose to charm us!—sometimes the sides of the mountains, along which we slowly wound our way, were covered with purple heath and yellow broom (the latter then beginning to shed their golden blossoms), mixed with the feathery fern, and creeping ivy; the fern grows also upon the trunks and branches of the cork trees, forming a singular effect of mingled foliage: at one time we passed green patches of land, kept as great trea-

---

* A moidore, at the present rate of exchange, is worth about three-and-twenty shillings.

sures for cattle to browze upon, where cows, climbing from steep to steep, were seen, each with a large bell around her neck—at another, our route led us by sparkling fountains of limpid water, " making music" to the ear of the thirsty pilgrim! —during this promenade, we alighted twice —once at the gates of the Marialva Palace, and once at those of the Pénha Verde (green rock), both of which we entered, and spent some time in walking over part of the romantic grounds of the latter. The Marialva belongs to the marquis of that name, (now banished, on account of his political opinions, from the country,) and is one of the chief lions of Cintra, being the favourite resort of all classes upon the evenings of Sundays or holidays. It is open at all times, and this reminds me of a very amiable feature in the Portugueze character—they always appear delighted to offer the sight or the use of their grounds to others, and receive your wish of exploring them, in the light of a compliment:—this has been confirmed to me by several English residents, and may afford a lesson to many of

60   CINTRA.

our own landed proprietors.   The Marialva is a fine looking building altogether,
and may probably be known in future times
from having been the place where the celebrated *Convention* was signed some years
since ; at least it will be remembered as long
as Childe Harold continues to be read !—
The gardens are rich, and the prospect the
windows command on both sides of the house
is magnificent. In spite of what is generally
acknowledged to be *good taste*, I could not
help being pleased with the contrast to the
wild simplicity of the general scene, which a
little old fashioned parterre in the front of
the mansion afforded : it was laid out in the
formal quaint style of our William the Third ;
and the sight of its straight close-shaven
hedges of yew and box, intersected at right
angles, together with a prim *jet d'eau* in
the centre, transported me in imagination to
Hampton Court, and brought those lines of
Pope to my remembrance, wherein he speaks
of that peculiar mode of planting.—

   " Grove nods at grove, each alley has a brother,
    And half the platform just reflects the other."

While I wondered at this coincidence of

táste, among the grandees of Portugal, (for almost *all* the large gardens of the nobility here are laid out in a similar manner,) I was informed that this place, as well as many others, was planned in the days when commerce flourished, the tutelar goddess of the land; and when merchants from *Holland*, in particular, resided and erected *mansions after their own hearts*, in the midst of Cintra's wildest *sérras;*—speaking of sérras, I could not resist giving a free rein to my fancy, during the most romantic part of our route; delighting to imagine myself in the heart of the " Sierra della Ronda," or in " the bowels of the Sable Mountain," mentioned in the exquisite descriptions of Spanish scenery by Cervantes—methought I could even see Sancho mounted upon Dapple, that " son of his soul," as he so pathetically calls him, and the gaunt " knight of the woeful countenance" extended at listless length beneath the shade of a hoary cork tree !—a flock of goats, ringing their bells as they descended from a distant height, conducted by some wild looking goat herds, so increased the illusion,

that I almost expected to behold the frantic
Cardenio among them!

I have hardly left myself room to mention the beautiful quinta of the Penha
Verde; so called, from a lofty mountain
rising immediately behind it, in the form
of a cone, covered to the utmost peak with
a luxuriant vegetation, that forms a fine
contrast to the bare and craggy rocks
which surround it.—This place originally
belonged to the celebrated hero, the virtuous Don João de Castro, (once governor-
general of India)—and to this peaceful retreat his fond thoughts perpetually recurred,
even amid the tumultuous scenes of war, and
all the splendours of the oriental world!—
The mansion at present is inhabited by another family; it is a good deal delapidated,
and I have heard it hinted that the neglected
state of the place has been in a great measure occasioned by the *gaming* propensities
of its proprietors; whether this be true or
not, I have no means of ascertaining—the
prevalence of this destructive pursuit is so
universal, that it is a common occurrence for
a young man of rank, in two years after

marriage, to find his affairs almost inextri-
cably involved; and this, even where his
wife has brought him a large dowry; to
extravagance of *other kinds* they are not so
prone. The fine woods belonging to Penha
Verde are so umbrageous, and are so eter-
nally refreshed by numerous fountains, that
it is possible to wander among them during
the most sultry hours of the day, without in-
curring either heat or fatigue; the grounds
are not devoid of the constant appendage to
every Portugueze quinta—a sort of terrace,
accommodated with seats, and shaded by
vines, myrtles, or other light foliage, raised
upon the wall which overlooks the public
road. *Here* the sénhoras delight to sit,
often in full dress, amusing themselves with
what *we* should be inclined to call the *vulgar*
occupation of watching for the appearance
of any chance passengers or equipages; in
the indulgence of this taste, (which is common, I believe, to most uneducated or idle
persons in *all* places,) they often consume
the principal portion of their time; and they
are reported to be remarkably satirical in
their comments upon those persons who

64   CINTRA.

happen to pass. On our return, we met a
family of peasants, consisting of an old but
hale cheerful looking grandmother, her two
daughters, and their children; they were
an interesting and picturesque group : the
infants soft skinned, dimpled, and dark-eyed;
and the young mothers really pretty : they
were all drest in the red petticoat and loose
linen jacket of the country, and actually appeared *clean;* but they were not so gay as a
village coquette whom I met a day or two
since, riding (as is customary here, completely sideways) upon her burinho ; her jacket
was laced in front with narrow gay coloured
ribbands, and she wore fine thread stockings worked like lace, and silk slippers embroidered with gold.   The Portugueze
have an amiable custom of saluting every
stranger who passes them either in walking
or riding—the upper classes bow courteous-
ly, and the lower generally exclaim " Viva !"
which kind wish is often accomcompanied
by a bright and friendly smile; this is beginning to decline, however, in the near
neighbourhood of the metropolis. The peasantry seem remarkably civil in their manner

to those above them, without any exhibition
of crouching servility; a muleteer, an almo-
creve, or a postilion who happens to meet you
in a narrow pass, will almost always take care
to annoy you as little as possible; still, I am
sorry to add, that in Lisbon, they behave by
no means so well.   The women now and then
ran out of their cottages after us, making
friendly signs, and beckoning with the two
middle fingers, in a manner peculiar to *all* the
Portugueze of whatever rank; this action
simply means to express " How do you do?"
some among them know as much English as
to *exclaim* " How do do ?" of which acquirement they appear very proud.   My little
boy excites much good will from all he
passes upon the road; they call out, "Bonito, muito bonito," (pretty, very pretty!)
and frequently attempt to caress him; indeed, I have once or twice been obliged
to prevent them from taking him up before
them upon their burinhos, as they ride to
market.   Three or four ancient beggars,
clad in weeds of every variety of colour,
and with long pastoral staves in their hands,
usually spend their time, basking in the

VOL. I.   F

66   CINTRA.

sun, upon a low stone wall in front of
our hotel; when I mounted my burinho
this morning, my boy remained for a few
minutes in the house, not being quite ready
to join me; upon which these hoary sires
inquired, with much appearance of disappointment, " where the little one was ?"—I
have met with few beggars in this neighbourhood, and those have never been troublesome or importunate; in Lisbon, however, they swarm about the door of every
shop, watching the coming out of the purchaser, whom they have followed thither
for the purpose of ascertaining that he has
furnished himself with small change; they
then assail him like mosquitos or hornets,
and are hardly to be repulsed till they have
obtained what they request. The manners
of women toward each other, are remarkably
caressante; the servant-girl of the hotel
at Buenos Ayres *kissed* my maid upon our
first arrival, as a matter of course, and the
abigail of a senhora now staying at Cintra,
in the same house with ourselves, never
meets her that she does not take hold of
both her hands, repeatedly kissing her upon

the cheek. The laundress we employ is a Moor; her dark skin and rolling eyes have a striking effect, half veiled in the ample white handkerchief which she has adopted in compliance with the native women in her class: upon being first introduced to me as her employer, I was in bed, and she gravely walked up to me, bowing in a courteous manner, and kissed my hand, saying, in good English, that she should take pleasure in serving my family; this custom is universal: all the servants of the house kiss the hand of the patrona (mistress), after every little absence on either side; and children, in some families, do the same to their parents, even upon quitting them for half an hour, repeating the same ceremony upon their return; there is a sort of patriarchal simplicity and cordiality in this, which is very attaching. The general honesty of the inhabitants of Cintra deserves mention; we are assured by persons who have resided forty years here, that an instance of house-breaking has not been known among them, and the inhabitants of the surrounding quintas hardly think it necessary to fasten their doors at

68   CINTRA.

night; with all this, however, they take
free license to cheat and impose in the way
of buying and selling; considering such
proceedings as mere *peccadinhos* (trifling
faults).   The children in Portugal, at least
those that I have seen, are usually pretty,
from the age of one to four years, and most
among the lower classes have the countenance, as well as the complexion of gipseys.

Drawn by M.Baillie.

PORTUGUEZE PEASANTS.

Published June, 1824, by John Murray, London.

CINTRA. **69**

LETTER X.

Cintra, July.

I DELIGHT in the peasantry here ; they are really a fine race of people, and if I understood their language sufficiently to converse with them, I have no doubt but I should think them almost as engaging as those of France. I must not forget to mention my daily attendant in all my rides, a lad about twelve or thirteen; poor fellow! nothing can exceed his readiness to oblige, and amuse me by every little method in his power; pointing out, with a faithful accuracy of taste, which, I should think, must in him be *intuitive*, the finest views and the most picturesque objects; stopping frequently on a sudden to make me observe a larger cork-tree than usual, a prettier quinta, or a more luxuriant hedge of myrtle or geranium: speaking of the former plant, I ought not to forget to tell you, that I have crossed a sort of wild common here, where the great-

70   CINTRA.

est variety of purple heaths bloomed in the
midst of an underwood, composed wholly of
myrtle bushes, and delicate arbutus trees,
in full flower and perfume !—My little guide
(to return to my first subject), however civil
and good tempered, is always secretly delighted when he has played me any *trick;*
the last time I went out, he struck into
a narrow path, which wound along the steep
side of a wooded mountain, surrounded by
craggy precipices, from which it was vain to
attempt any retreat; enjoying my glances
of surprise and dismay, as the burinho, doub-
ling his hind legs underneath his body, *slid*
down the abrupt descents, and bursting
into an inexpressible shout of mirth, as the
animal plunged with me into a shallow ford
at the bottom, through which, nevertheless,
it carried me with ease and safety; but this
ridiculous imp amused me so much, that I
forgot half my terrors ; grinning till I could
have numbered every one of his white teeth,
he vaulted from crag to crag, with admira-
ble agility; dashing on,

> " Through mud, through mire,
>   Over bush and over briar,"

and never losing sight of my countenance,
which he watched with all the roguish ma-
lice of a will-o'-the-wisp, or a "goblin page :"
at the termination of the adventure, which
carried us at least seven or eight miles from
home, this brat did not appear in the least
fatigued, but came running up to assist me
in dismounting, biting his lips to prevent
laughing, and evidently full of triumph at
the joke he had ventured, yet endeavouring
to assume a face of gravity and officious
respect, as he inquired, " at what hour
the senhora chose to employ him the next
day?"

Count F. and Baron d'O., the Prussian
minister and secretary of legation at the
court of the Brazils, lately arrived in
this country, have been passing a few days
at the hotel here, and were indefatigable
in *lionizing;* they are the most agreeable persons we have met with since we
entered Portugal, and as Mr. B. is now
returned from Lisbon, I have been able
to join their society at dinner every day.
An anecdote which they told us, relative
to a fair *penitent* of the Roman Catholic

persuasion, which occurred while they
were at Rio Janeiro, is too ludicrous to be
omitted in this letter: I think it will
amuse you as much as it has done ourselves.

A reverend father confessor was one day
gravely seated in his confessional, listening
to the peccadinhos of a poor negress, whose
chief failing was that of drunkenness; the
confessor, as she was rather *prolix* in her
acknowledgments, took the opportunity of
going very comfortably to sleep, secure in
his snug retreat of not being observed by
any prying or profane eye; the negress,
having finished what she had to say, waited
a considerable time in expectation of receiving absolution; but finding that the holy
father remained silent, concluded that he
was too much shocked at her enormities to
speak, and, with a deep sigh, she quietly
withdrew from the grate, and went out of
the church.   At the same moment, the
Senhora (somebody), the young and handsome wife of one of the richest merchants
in the country arrived, took possession of
the vacant space, and began to confess *her*

sins to the same worthy auditor: she had
hardly begun, when the latter, suddenly
awakening from his nap, and concluding the
negress to be still at the grate, commenced,
in *his* turn, a severe reprimand upon the
subject of her drunken propensities: nothing could equal the indignation of the
Senhora; conceiving herself to be the
person really addressed, she launched forth
in the most furious manner; venting her
wrath at what she called the " infamous
calumnies" of the priest, in language too
gross to repeat.

We are more and more amazed, the longer we remain in this country, at that ignorance, or, at best, that *superficial* knowledge
of the commonest arts which exist among
the Portugueze; a carpenter here is the
awkwardest and most clumsy artizan that
can be imagined, spoiling every work he
attempts; the way in which the doors
and other wood-work belonging even to
good houses are finished, would really have
suited the rudest ages! Their carriages of
all kinds (more particularly their waggons
and carts), their agricultural implements and

74   CINTRA.

management, their cutlery, locks and keys, &c., are *ludicrously* bad; their soil, rich and fertile, their climate so favourable to the growth of almost all vegetation, seems, in a great measure, to be lost upon them; and, in short (if I am to judge by the little I have seen, and to credit entirely what others tell me), the state of society, and the progress of civilization in all classes, are so infinitely below par, so strikingly inferior to the rest of Europe, as to form a sort of disgraceful wonder in the midst of the nineteenth century: what can be the reason of this peculiarity? There are not wanting persons who decidedly account for it upon the score of an extraordinary self-conceit, similar to that of the Chinese nation, than which, nothing can be a more sure bar to improvement: I would fain hope this judgment is too severe.

CINTRA. **75**

LETTER XI.

Cintra, July.

WE have this evening been to see the quinta of "Montserrat," by far the most picturesque place in this neighbourhood; it comprises every beauty and sublimity which Cintra has to boast, being situated upon very elevated ground, in the bosom of a wood of cork-trees, surrounded by orange-trees, and rocky fountains; hemmed in on three sides by mountains, (among which are those crowned by the Penha convent, and the Moorish castle,) and open on the other to the level champaign country, rich in vineyards and cornfields, which stretches out for about six miles, when it is bounded by the sea. The mansion itself had a singular charm for me, delighting, as I have ever done, in those which call up images of romantic association; it was originally built by a rich Englishman,* in the style of our own villas, and was in consequence distinguished by an elegance of taste, a refinement of de-

* Mr. Beckford, of Fonthill.

76   CINTRA.

coration, and a lightness and beauty of architecture, which are peculiar to buildings
of this sort in England; *here* such a structure really appears as if raised by fairy
hands; so far does it excel the ill-contrived
and tawdry style, to which the natives of this
country are generally accustomed;—but,
alas! how has this enchanted spot been
neglected! and how has the beautiful house
been suffered to fall to decay! now become the property of a Portugueze family,
they have evinced the most deplorable want
of taste and feeling in regard to it, for at this
moment it is completely a ruin—a fit residence only for the bat and the owl, or to
serve as a casual shelter for the wandering
goatherd and his shaggy flock, at those
times when the wind is not high enough to
blow down the shattered roof upon their
heads. I never beheld so striking an image
of desolate loveliness; and could have
passed hours here in the indulgence of a
reverie, mournful, yet fraught with a name-
less charm that can only be comprehended
by the veritable children of romance. Some
of the carved doors of the best apartments

(brought, at a great expense, from England), were still perfect, and some remains of the superb plates of glass in the light French windows were yet spared by the fury of the wintry storms which often rage with great violence among the surrounding mountains and woods; the hall (of Grecian elegance) once opened upon a sloping lawn of verdant turf, studded with rare shrubs and flower-beds; it has now been ploughed up, but I could still discover traces of its former designation; a splendid music-room, built in the form of a rotunda, the roof rising in a fine dome, to a considerable height, made the greatest impression upon my feelings; I tried my voice there, and was startled at the sound, which, as it died away, seemed to scare the long sleeping echoes of the place. Montserrat indeed is well calculated to afford a lesson of philosophy to every being who has *learnt to think;* here, in the days of its splendour, its original proprietor retired, to enjoy the luxuries of almost boundless wealth, and called around him the sons and daughters of prosperity, to enliven the retreats of a hitherto solitary

78   CINTRA.

Eden; *now*, what a change, and what a
contrast!

As the national character of the Portugueze gradually unfolds itself to our observation, we sometimes smile, but more frequently sigh with a feeling of deeper and
more serious import: from all we have
been able to gather, to hear, and to remark,
nothing can be more deplorable than the
state of morality, civil polity, and religion
(generally considered), in which they have
hitherto remained: and there has not yet
been time for any great or radical improvement, since the accession of a more liberal
form of government: with respect to religion, however, I shall not mention much
which I have been told concerning it; for,
being myself a Protestant, I may be suspected of prejudice in judging of an opposite
persuasion.

Justice is said to be too frequently bought
and sold; indeed, it is not to be expected, that,
having an "itching palm," she should hold the
sword with a firm and steady grasp. Many
horrid crimes,—murder one of the most
venial among them—are frequently com-

mitted, almost with impunity; nor are the
perpetrators banished from general society!
A man has just assassinated his wife, under
circumstances of the most aggravated cruelty, and in cold blood, after long and ma-
ture deliberation; he had several children
by the unfortunate woman, and he committed the savage act, almost before their
eyes! she was not guiltless in her conduct,
but he had ever afforded her an example of
licentiousness and infidelity: after having
been convicted upon the clearest evidence,
he is only punished by imprisonment at present, nor is it thought probable that he will
ever be brought to actual execution.*

All Roman Catholic countries observe the
Sunday in a manner which, to an English
eye, does not appear exactly the most appropriate to the sacred character of the day;
but in Portugal, I think they seem to pay
still less reverence to it, than in any other!
I cannot forbear the relation of the following
circumstance, which may be offered as my
best excuse for this severity of opinion.

* He was liberated before we left Lisbon.

80 CINTRA.

The day before yesterday I went into a church here, to witness the celebration of mass on Sunday morning; the service itself did not last above half an hour, and there was but one officiating priest, who muttered it over in so hurried and indistinct a manner, that it would have been impossible for even the *learned* to have understood or followed him! He gave the sacrament to one communicant, and as soon as the ceremony was over, he wiped out the cup, and then set himself (in view of every person present) busily to work, rubbing and polishing its outside surface, with a cloth, exactly with the air of a butler who was particularly tenacious of the lustre of his sideboard. There was no sermon, and although the gallery was provided with an organ, we heard not a note of music. The high altar, with all its ornaments, was *covered up*, and the service performed before another very shabby little one, in the side of the church. Upon inquiring *why* all this had occurred? I was answered with much composure, " that it was troublesome to uncover and dress out the high altar *merely for Sunday*, or to have

music; but that on some *Saints'* days, both
were to be seen and heard in great splendour
and perfection."

We dined lately at the quinta of an American merchant here, a very rich individual,
who has resided many years·in Portugal. At
this house we met several foreigners, and were
introduced to a Portugueze family, who were
accompanied by their two young children.
I was assured, that it is generally the custom
to bring them to balls, parties, &c. at the most
tender age; by which means, late hours are
inevitably induced, and these (joined to the
want of exercise peculiar to the inhabitants
of Lisbon) render the little beings invariably
delicate, and frequently unhealthy!

In the course of the evening we went to
view the *interior* of the Marialva, which is,
in fact, no paláce properly so called, but a
large country mansion, which has hitherto
been preserved in tolerably good repair.
As we wandered through the spacious apartments, where now and then a piece of neat
English furniture contrasted advantageously
with the general foreign style of decoration,
we were struck by the superiority of the

manner in which the walls of every room
were painted in fresco. This is the only
thing in which I think the Portugueze taste
better than our own,—the delicacy and
beauty of the colouring, and the variety of
the designs, (the latter copied from antique
patterns chiefly of flowers,) were far preferable to the most elaborate French papers;
and although Italian artists are sometimes
employed, the Portugueze themselves are
very happy in the execution of this style of
decoration, which is nearly universal both
in Lisbon and in the country.

I observe not unfrequently a black cross,
of rude workmanship, erected in different
parts of the neighbourhood, and am told,
that such is the signal that either a murder
has been committed, or some fatal accident
has happened upon that particular spot.
A symbol of this melancholy nature is more
than usually conspicuous in one of the wildest
and most beautiful places in the vicinity,
and forms an object of romantic pilgrimage
to almost all strangers; it is planted above
a mossy bank of earth, called " The Lover's
Grave," where, in effect, the bodies of three

unfortunates are buried, whose sad story, in
spite of the long lapse of time since the
event occurred, is yet fresh in the memory
of every village maiden. It is soon told :—
" Two youthful brothers once happily *lived*
amid the sylvan shades which now resound
with lamentations for their untimely *deaths.*
They were each brave, and beautiful; and
their fraternal affection was the theme of
every tongue. The elder formed an attachment to a lovely girl, whose family, if I recollect aright, were somewhat averse to their
union. In a moment of more than ordinary
vexation, she appointed the *younger* brother
to meet her in a certain woody glen, in order
to consult with him upon the means of sur-
mounting the difficulties in which she found
herself involved, upon account of her constant attachment to the elder, whose more
fiery temperament was less calculated to
reason dispassionately and with due prudence, upon so touching a subject! They
met—the youth suggested a plan which
appeared to the fair and animated creature
so admirably suited to effect her wishes,
that she embraced him in all the warmth of

84   CINTRA.

sisterly gratitude.   Alas! the impetuous
lover had beheld, from a distance, and in
the gloom of twilight, his mistress in the
arms of—a *stranger,* as he unfortunately
imagined; maddened by jealousy, he rushed
forward, and plunged his dagger in the heart
of his brother! The mistake was explained
in a moment, and the unhappy youth completed the tragedy by stabbing himself
upon the. body of his guiltless victim.   The
lady survived not long, and they were all
interred beneath the same ensanguined
turf!" I will not vouch for the accuracy of
every particular of this tale of woe; but the
outlines at least are correct, and I leave it to
your own imagination to fill them up in the
manner you like best.

                                      Adieu.

LETTER XII.

Cintra, July 30th.

I HAVE as yet, had no opportunity of forming any individual judgment, respecting the modes and morals of the higher classes of society; and the answers I receive upon *inquiry* into these circumstances, are so un-favourable, that I feel considerable reluctance to believe the half of what I hear! It is an undoubted truth however, that the decency and decorum of *outward appearances* are always sedulously preserved; much more so, than in our own country, and this from the highest to the lowest orders of people. Even in the worst haunts of Lisbon, little *external* mark of depravity, or even impropriety, is ever visible; what are we to think of this peculiar feature in the national character? for my own part, although I fear that it evinces a great proficiency in the art of de-ception, I am of opinion, that it is preferable to a more open display of immorality; and

86   CINTRA.

it certainly illustrates the truth of the well
known axiom, "that hypocrisy is the in-
voluntary homage which vice pays to virtue."
Perhaps some moralists might be startled at
this decision; and I allow that it may be
combated, without any degree of illiberality
or injustice. Doubtless it is far better " to
be what we *seem*," yet I cannot but think
many really excellent persons amongst *us*
might borrow a useful hint, from the fair
exterior of the Portugueze, and they would
do well to remember, in the midst of their
overstrained sincerity, that by the needless
harshness of outward manners, virtue herself
may be rendered unlovely; an amiable and
truly exemplary author, who is now no more,
has well observed upon this subject, " that
it is high treason against religion and morality, to be good and disagreeable!"

Street robbery is almost as common in
Lisbon as in London, but there is this fatal
difference, peculiar to the Portugueze delin-
quent; " he hardly ever robs, without
assassination." Dishonesty and petty theft
flourish here in as rank luxuriance as can
well be imagined; nor can confidence be

placed in any persons so surely, as in the humble hardworking sort of voluntary slaves, called "gallegos," who hire out their strength and activity to the more indolent natives. The rude honesty of these Spaniards may (it is universally asserted) be trusted with untold gold; they resemble in many of their habits and offices, the *Cawdies* of Edinburgh, and the Lazzaroni of Naples. I forget whether I have already mentioned to you, that they come over in immense bodies, from the province of Gallicia in Spain; live on their journey here upon the charitable daily dole of the convents, and carefully hoarding the money which they obtain for their hard-earned services, return when they have made a certain sum, to their own country, to spend their latter years in the bosoms of their families: most of them are remarkably athletic, and I have observed that the younger among them, are sometimes extremely fine men.

Having recovered from a transient attack of rheumatism, which I am told is one of the

88   CINTRA.

drawbacks to enjoyment, *peculiar* to the
humid climate of Cintra, I went at a very
early hour this morning, to drink the cool
water of a fountain, (said to be slightly im-
pregnated with iron,) in the beautiful gardens
of a quinta hard by, where the chestnut and
young cork trees grow so thickly, as to form
an impervious shade, even during the hottest
hours of the day.   Here I spent half an
hour, listening to the cool gushing sound of
the fountain, and the soft monotonous note
of the wood pigeon, which builds among
these quiet haunts.   I was soon joined by a
companion, who had passed many years in
Portugal, and she gave me the history of the
owner of the quinta, which was not uninteresting.   He is a very young man, but
has been for some years a husband and a
father, having married (according to the
national custom) in boyhood, a girl of thirteen or fourteen, who is said to have united
a premature perfection of person, to a disposition wild, thoughtless, and uncontrouled,
beyond all belief; spoiled by early adula-
tion, she had no idea—no care, unconnected
with either her beauty or her amusement:

CINTRA. **89**

at length, jealousy, on the part of the youthful husband, (although vague, and devoid
of any definite object,) arose, to complete
his uneasiness, and, in a moment of irritation,
he suddenly shut her up in one of those
religious houses, which in this country are
appropriated to the reception of separated
wives who have given cause of scandal to
society. Such power has the Romish church
hitherto allowed to husbands in general!
In these melancholy retreats, though bound
by no vow or profession, these unfortunate
women are condemned to remain, until set
at liberty by the relenting feelings of their
husbands, or (what is often far more welcome)
by their *deaths*. In this durance, the fair
lady of the quinta still resides, while her
lord continues to lead a solitary and listless
life, untouched as yet by compassion for
her fate: he is frequently encountered wandering amid these shades, looking (doubtless) extremely " sentimental, melancholy
and gentlemanlike." I forgot to ask my
informant, whether these penitential prisons
were likely to be suppressed by the Constitutional government; but I learnt another

90   CINTRA.

piece of intelligence, at which I could not
but heartily rejoice, " that the different
orders of nuns and friars were henceforward
to be abolished; that the communities at
present in existence were to be allowed to
die a natural death, while all attempts at
future revival would be punished with severity." This appears to be one of the most
wholesome of the new regulations; yet I
ought not to forget the final destruction of
the Inquisition, which the present ministers
have effected. The infernal dominion of
this institution has been declining for a considerable period of time; and most persons
have allowed themselves to imagine, that its
worst atrocities had come to a conclusion,
long previous to the recent Revolution;
but in this supposition, I was assured that
they had been greatly mistaken: for only
a few months have elapsed, since several
instances of the most detestable cruelty and
injustice are said to have been brought to
light, which but too plainly evinced, that the
original character of the inquisition was by
no means changed.

I have lately heard several anecdotes of

the past enormities of the priesthood in
general, (and relating more particularly to
the members of a certain rich and noble
convent,) which I shall not repeat; they may
or may not be true, but at all events it is
painful to contemplate human nature in such
fearful colours as those to which they allude:
one however, of a milder character, I will
relate to you; for its simplicity well deline-
ates the state of opinion among the common
people, in respect to subjects connected
with religion. An English lady (herself a
liberal, though sincere Roman Catholic)
had of late attempted to *reason* with some
of the peasantry (whose milder dispositions
allowed her to venture upon doing so, without risk of their resentment), and to point
out to them the absurdity of their prayers
when addressed to *saints*—(to have told
them that such a practice was in reality
forbidden by the Apostles in the Gospel,
would have been fruitless; because the
Scriptures, entire and unadulterated, are for
ever concealed from their perusal, by the
priests of their peculiar church!)—one of
these rustics, in reply, expressed the uni-

versal sentiment prevalent among them. " It
is proper and right, (said he,) to apply to
the saints, when we want any thing; they
are in favour with God, and can (if they are
pleased with our offerings) obtain for us
every good gift.   With regard to addressing
ourselves to God himself, that would be a
very *unwise* method of proceeding; would
any prudent person present a request to the
king, when he knows that his ear is open only
to the persuasions and representations of
the fidalgos who surround him? now the
saints are *God's* fidalgos, and therefore we
pray to *them*."   What a blind and unworthy
idea of the attributes of our Great Creator,
must these poor people entertain! but we
should not condemn them too severely; for
the above instance proves, that at least the sin
of *Pharisaical presumption* (too common
with some Protestants) is not imputable to
them!   There is another superstition also,
which deserves mention, relative to the *host;*
when this sacred emblem is sent for, upon
the summons of a sick person, divers prog-
nostics are always formed, from the number
of persons who voluntarily follow the pro-

cession to the door of the penitent; if *many,* the person will recover; if a *few,* his illness will be of a very dangerous nature: but when the attendant priests *only* are seen, unaccompanied by any lay spectators, the event, it is infallibly pronounced, will be *fatal!* How horrible is the custom which universally prevails here, of suffering the street door to remain open, to the intrusion of every rude and careless observer; when beggars and children have frequently been known to penetrate unchidden, into the very chamber of the dying person, where they are allowed to stare upon the agonies of the sufferer, and to disturb the sacred grief of the surviving relatives! Adieu.

———

94   CINTRA.

LETTER XIII.

Cintra, August 3d.

THE Portugueze government has hitherto
been generally censured for an excess of
bigotry, unknown among other continental
nations.   I am inclined however to think,
it is not worse than what *now* exists among
the French; (if we judge from the conduct
pursued by the latter towards Protestants,
even as lately as during the years 1815 and
1816, in the south of France, mentioned by
Mr. Wilks) nor am I without a strong
hope, that the sentiment is here beginning
very rapidly to wear away, among *all* classes
of people.   Individual instances to the con-
trary are at the same time frequently to be
met with; I myself heard the pope's nuncio,
at present in the neighbourhood of this
place, very rigorously and bitterly spoken
of, as a faithless recreant to his holy profession and office, merely because he was
casually met tranquilly walking in the cool

of the evening, among these beautiful scenes
of romantic nature, in the society of an English married lady of a certain age, whose
reputation for propriety of conduct in every
respect stood particularly high; and this
too, when there were one or two more
persons in company! It was stated, by his
censors, that it was against the rules of his
church, to mingle in the society of females.
Another instance of a similar contraction of
mind, I cannot help mentioning; it has in
the latter case so completely silenced the
soft voice of pleading humanity, as to induce
a family of the Romish religion, now resident in Portugal, still to regard with feelings
of unmingled *abhorrence* the venial trespass
of a young girl, who, about twenty years
since, committed in their eyes an *inexpiable*
crime against Heaven, in flying from a convent where she had been detained *against
her inclinations!* A circumstance of a most
horrible nature, which occurred during her
confinement in that place, so greatly increased her inherent dislike of a conventual
life, that she refused at the end of her pro-
bation to assume the final veil; her rela-

96 CINTRA.

tions however, were inexorable, and, in the
extremity of her distress, she made a confi-
dant of her married sister, whose liberal
ideas of true religion had induced her to
unite her fate to that of an English protestant, and who, in consequence of this union,
had lost in a great degree the affection and
countenance of her family. This friendly
and compassionate couple concerted the
mode of their youthful sister's escape; a
lady, who was going to England, was admitted to a participation of the secret, and
she kindly undertook to carry her off in her
own suite, under the disguise of a servant,
the captain of the vessel having previously
agreed to favour her evasion by receiving
her on board; but alas! when the moment
of active exertion arrived, and the trembling victim claimed his services, coming in
an open boat to the ship's side, he allowed
his fears of the Inquisition to get the better
of his honour, and had actually the in-
humanity to refuse her admittance; but
the gallant conduct of the officers belonging
to another English ship made amends for
this cruel disappointment: one of them

came on shore the same evening, and calling
upon the married sister, remarked the agitation of her spirits; she entrusted the
secret to his compassionate ear, and he, with
the gallant ardour peculiar to an Englishman, at once undertook to carry the fugitive
safely to England, and to deliver her as soon as
possible into the care of the lady to whom I
have already alluded : in fact, so energetic
and prompt were his measures, that the first
object which the anxious sister beheld the
next morning, upon rising, was the ship,
with its full sails spread, and the well known
colours of England floating in the breeze,
having already gained the farthest extremity
of the Tagus, bearing rapidly away from
the shores of Portugal! she seized a tele-
scope, and after a short period of harrowing
suspense, had the happiness of beholding
it *pass the bar*, where launching out into
the free ocean, it was soon out of the reach
of suspicion or pursuit! The whole affair
was managed with singular prudence and
address, for no distrust subsequently attached to the contrivers of the escape; had this
been otherwise, they would inevitably have

98   CINTRA.

fallen victims to the resentment of the Inquisition: the fugitive arrived safely in
that generous country, so often the refuge
of the persecuted and afflicted, and was
afterwards happily married to a man of
good fortune.   The circumstance at which
I hinted in the commencement of this story,
which so much aggravated the horror of
the young novice, would form a fit subject
for a melancholy romance. A lady, not
many years older than herself, with whom
she had contracted a passionate friendship,
had been compelled by the intrigues of her
relations, to break off a marriage with a
deserving object to whom she was deeply
attached, and to take the veil, in the same
convent.   The means adopted, to effect
this sacrifice, were fabricated accounts of
the infidelity of the lover; she had scarcely
pronounced the extorted vow, ere the young
man found means to convince her of the
falsehood of all which had been alleged
against him; and the lady, after infinite
combats, between affection for her lover and
dread of discovery, at length formed the
desperate resolution of escaping with him

from the convent, intending, should their plan succeed, to fly to some more happier and more liberal country, where they might be united.—Alas! she was discovered, and condemned to be inclosed between two walls, in the same manner with *Constance* in the poem of Marmion, there to endure a lingering aud miserable death by inanition! While her previous trial was still going on, which lasted for several weeks, she was immured in a cell, situated in a remote part of the convent; her more fortunate young friend had at this time nearly finished her noviciate: she had been attacked with an indisposition which confined her to her own cell, during the performance of this tragedy, and upon inquiring, after her recovery, for the senhora, was told by the superior, that she had suddenly expired. Some days afterwards, in the height of her regret, as she was accidentally passing the before mentioned cell of despair, she was startled by a faint groan; it burst from the overcharged bosom of the person she so fondly lamented! She knew the voice, and in a moment, was made acquainted with the whole of her companion's sad story. From that evening, she contrived (by means too tedious to relate) to effect frequent meetings, and here the unhappy friends used to pass many an undiscovered moment of melancholy conversation. " Adieu, my dear Flora," said the captive, one night, upon taking leave of her companion in misfortune, at the usual hour, " I fear we shall never meet again! I have a presentiment that I speak to you for the last time." The event too fatally justified her mysterious words; for upon her cell being opened the following morning, she was found lifeless, drowned in her own blood, having destroyed herself in an access of despair. It is dreadful to think of the abuse of power which has until now existed in this church. Formerly, whole families of younger children were perpetually sacrificed, and compelled to wear out their life in the austere seclusion of a cloister, merely to aggrandize the elder son; and I am assured that it has repeatedly happened, that Portugueze youths, thus persecuted, have no sooner taken the forced vows required of them, than they have once more knelt,

CINTRA.   **101**

before the same profaned altar, for the
purpose of swearing (in secret) to take the
most horrible methods of revenge upon their
tyrants, even though the latter were the
authors of their existence! Revenge has
long been asserted by universal report, to
be a leading feature in the character of this
people; another, is said to be the sudden
and extreme irascibility of their temper,
upon comparatively slight provocation; the
latter appears, from all we have been able
to gather, to be wearing away; but the
former still continues to manifest itself in
the basest and most cowardly manner.
There is a village on the shores of the
Tagus, near Lisbon, consisting of rude huts,
inhabited solely by the families of fishermen,
where both qualities are sometimes carried
to a tremendous excess. These people are
represented to us, as being almost in a savage
state: they keep themselves distinct from
all other classes, and in consequence of their
hardy active mode of life, the bracing influence of the sea air, and the effect of better
food than is usually enjoyed by the peasantry, (as they always get good bread and

102   CINTRA.

fresh fish,) are a remarkably athletic fine
race.   Their mud-walled huts, covered with
reeds, or straw, (somewhat resembling those
of the lower Irish,) are built upon
heaps of sand and shingle, and washed by
a surge, which frequently dashes against
the rocky shore, with the most awful
grandeur, and angry force.   It is accounted
rather hazardous to visit this colony,
the inhabitants being so easily offended;
and when one of them only is provoked, it
is usual for the whole community to rush
out to his assistance, and to support his
cause, (whether just or otherwise,) by the
powerful eloquence of clubs and stones:
their children are remarkably handsome,
generally speaking, and wilder than the free-
born winds and waves!   The parents themselves are often fine models of fierce beauty
and strength; I have seen a family of them,
who formed the most picturesque group
I ever beheld: the husband, bronzed by
his frequent buffeting against sun and
storm, had regular, *well chiselled* features,
teeth white as snow, dark flashing eyes,
deepset, and shaded by a heavy fall of

shadowy lashes, and marked brows, whose expression was that of determined hardihood and independence of spirit: his hair, of the deepest shade of sunny brown, played round his face, and fell in long thick ringlets upon his shoulders. The wife rose rather above the middle height of women; her figure, without being in the smallest degree bony, or clumsy in its proportions, was the perfection of springing energy and healthful vigour; and I particularly remarked the beauty of her naked legs and feet, which might have emulated those of an Atalanta: upon her head, gracefully erect, she carried a large heavy pitcher, apparently without effort, balancing it, devoid of any assistance from her hands, which were employed in bearing a basket, and some of the fishing nets: her features (particularly when viewed in profile) were delicately formed, upon the true Greek model, while her cheeks pale as marble, and of a beautiful oval contour, gave her altogether an appearance of classical elegance; their children played around them; dark eyed, sallow, yet not uninteresting little urchins, one of them with rich curled hair like that of the father, and all of them nearly destitute of clothing of any sort: we saw (at a distance) the hamlet to which they belonged, at the time when we first entered the harbour of Lisbon. One of the fishermen came on board our vessel, with fish to sell, habited in his gala costume, as it was the eve of the festival of St. John. I did not think it either ungraceful or ill-chosen; the chief peculiarity lay in the bright scarlet vest or waistcoat, ornamented profusely with small gilt buttons of a filligree pattern, resembling those worn at Talavera in Spain. This *worthy* had an acute sharp expression of countenance, and piercing black eyes, which were always in quick and restless motion, and placed so near together in the head, that they conveyed the idea of a monkey to my mind; his fish was excellent; but he attempted (*as usual*, we were told) to impose most outrageously upon the purchaser.

You are to remember, that all these digressive anecdotes have arisen from the original conversation which in the beginning of my letter, I was holding with you, upon

CINTRA. **105**

the subject of Portugueze bigotry. I have rambled widely from the former path, and know not how to regain it with propriety; yet I have still something more to say upon that topic—I will reserve it for another opportunity.

106   CINTRA.

LETTER XIV.

Cintra, August.

THE shady solitude of the quinta of the
fountain is become my daily resource.   I
lately heard a droll anecdote of the *village
poet,* here, who frequently comes to drink
of the same salubrious waters; whether
they answer *his* purpose as well as those of
Helicon, I know not; but *I* have experienced the cacoëthes scribendi in a greater
degree than usual, since I have accustomed
myself to their use; you shall have one of
my reveries in rhyme, by this letter; but
first I must go on with my anecdote respecting the bard of Cintra, for whom I have
often been on the watch, expecting to see
him wandering about, (as I then supposed,)
like melancholy Jaques, pondering by the
mossy brink of the fountain, or muttering
his wayward fancies to the woods and

rocks; but my interest is now quite extinct; for I have heard that he is so far unlike a true son of the Muse, (who should live chiefly upon *air*,) as to be a great glutton, and more particularly fond of plumpudding: Poetry and pudding! what a horrible alliteration! they ought always to be kept " far as the poles asunder." This personage is rather a mauvais sujet, and has of late fallen into fresh disgrace, upon account of a little bourgeoise from Lisbon, who is staying for her health, under the hospitable protection of a Scotch catholic family, now resident in Cintra. With this little monkey, (for although forward enough in some respects, her age does not reach fourteen,) he had struck up a fierce flirtation, which went on unheeded by the family, for some time; but it was now and then remarked, that the sweetmeats, fruit, cakes, and other dainties, vanished from the pantry, in a most unaccountable way; at length, the secret was unravelled, by the housekeeper, one luckless morning, at peep of dawn, who pounced upon the young lady, just as she was dismissing *the poet*, from the door of

108   CINTRA.

the house, after a tender farewell embrace, who on his part had his mouth (not his *heart*) too full to reply to this pathetic demonstration of affection! in his hand, were the last remains of a fried plumpudding, which had been missed, as usual, the night before. The sequel may easily be imagined. The damsel is to be sent back to Lisbon, the poet has returned to his accustomed slender fare, and the pantry has been padlocked, ever since. I know not whether the present is not rather an unfavourable moment to introduce my lucubration, which was, I assure you, the offspring of real melancholy, and depression of spirit. Be assured however, that if these impressions were not *transient*, and proceeding partly from physical causes, I should not run the risk of paining you, by thus offering their expression to your sight.

THE EXILE'S LAMENT.

Yes! lovely is this foreign land;
Sublime the mountain, fair the vale;
Rich are yon òrange groves, and bland
The perfumed breath of every gale.

CINTRA.   **109**

Then wherefore sinks my wayward heart?
What means this ever rising sigh?
Can scenes like these, no joys impart?
What wouldst thou more? sad heart, reply!

'Tis *home* alas! that I desire,
Thither my absent spirit strays,
While on my trembling lips expire,
Th' unconscious words of hollow praise!

While here I rest in myrtle bowers,
O'ershadowed by the purple vine,
I sadly think on happier hours,
That once 'midst humbler shades, were mine!

And when the foreign tongue I hear,
Or on the stranger's visage dwell,
I turn to hide the ready tear,
And check the grief I may not tell!

No well-known voice to me replies,
No parent's look of love I meet,
No friend's warm smile can bless my eyes;
The wandering Exile, who shall greet?

Here, 'mid these scenes, so " rich and rare,"
With wild romantic beauty blest,
Foul murder stalks, with sullen stare,
And vice unblushing, rears her crest!

110   CINTRA.

Here superstition reigns supreme,
Absolving deeds of sin and shame;
Here slothful monks supinely dream,
Disgracing sweet religion's name!

Surrounded by a listless race,
The sallow children of the soil,
'Tis rare the ruddy cheek I trace
Of labour, warm with healthful toil.

I view the straw-roof'd cot no more,
Where industry and neatness dwell;
No trim-kept garden's fragrant store,
Here tempts the bee to build her cell!

Oh! I am sick of many a grief,
To hard ambitious hearts unknown;
Wealth's futile hope gives no relief;
What would I then?—my home alone!

Smit with the thought of home, I pine;
Nor absent, know the name of joy,
Save when I think that still are mine,
My husband and my blooming boy.

Oh that within our country's breast,
To us a tranquil home were giv'n,
Where we from life's rude storms might rest,
And gently steal from earth to Heav'n!

LETTER XV.

Cintra, August.

SOME customs of the Portugueze appear
strange indeed, in the eyes of an English
person! The manner in which young
children are fed, particularly surprizes me;
their food (more especially for breakfast)
consists of a sort of pap, composed of bread,
water, garlic, and oil; the latter (made in
this country) is uniformly strong and rancid,
as they prefer it of that flavour, to the fine
Florence or Lucca oils, saying " those have
no taste." Oil of another sort is nevertheless produced, from their native olive, which
is pure and excellent; but this, for the same
reason, is generally undervalued among all
classes. The Portugueze imagine this worse
than Spartan broth, to be remarkably wholesome, and appropriate to the delicacy of an
infant's stomach! Then the quantity of
cold water, which most people drink during

112   CINTRA.

the day, is beyond all belief; I am afraid
to mention it, lest I should be suspected of
the well known fault of *travellers!* Women,
in the higher and middling classes, (and
people, more particularly foreigners, who
come to settle here,) suffer a great
deal from weakness of digestion, and other
disorders, incident to a sedentary mode of
life.   Embonpoint, or rather decided fat, is
greatly admired; and some people imagine
that the habit of swallowing such large
draughts of water, (provoked in some
measure by the quantity of luscious sweetmeats they eat,) produces this effect; sugar
being generally allowed to fatten the human
frame; but then what a fat! white, unwholesome, and devoid of that firmness, which
belongs to health alone! I have seen figures
which appeared as if in the last stage of
a dropsy, and I cannot conceive how persons
in their senses, can think or call them beautiful.

A lady, whose visit I returned this morning, had lately taken a ramble in the mountains, to see the celebrated Cork convent,
mentioned by every body who has ever

resided in the neighbourhood of Cintra. She was shocked at the humidity of the cells, appointed for the brotherhood, which rather resemble the lairs of wild beasts, than habitations proper for the abode of human creatures; speaking the language with fluency, she entered into conversation with one of the monks, a young man, who appeared out of health, and very melancholy. She inquired if he was *dull* in this sequestered and gloomy residence? to which he replied with a sigh, " I am not very happy, certainly!" " Let me intreat you to answer me with candour," pursued his inquisitive visitor; " did you enter this community of your own accord, or were you forced into taking the vows?" " Alas!" said he, " my parents dedicated me to a monastic life, when I was in the cradle!" This has been but too common, both in Spain and Portugal. The little victims, when able to walk, are immediately clothed in miniature habits of the order of monks to which they are destined to belong, and which they constantly wear; I myself have seen a little boy, (the younger son of a noble family,) with the

VOL. I. I

114 CINTRA.

crown of his head shaven, as he was intended
for the priesthood. The poor monk of the
Cork convent has *now* an opportunity of
quitting his austere confinement, if he wishes
to do so; but most probably he has never
learnt any thing which might be of *use* to
him in the world, has acquired habits of
indolence which would unfit him from earn-
ing a subsistence, and his health is (as the
lady described,) ruined by the absurd pri-
vations imposed upon him, by a perverted
idea of religious duty. The brothers of this
order are not allowed to eat meat at any
time, and they fast often, even from their
usual scanty fare; that they do *sometimes*
break through so needless a prohibition, is
however well known; the same lady, whose
talent for cross-questioning was equal to
that of a lawyer, inquired of the young man,
" whether it was forbidden also for them to
dress meat?" " No," said he, nothing is
said against our *cooking* meat,"—" you now
and then *dress* it I suppose?"—" yes, very
seldom." "And after it is drest, what happens
then?"—" Oh, we—certainly we *do* go a step
farther, and *eat* it also; but very rarely, as

I have told you before, for it is against our rules, and therefore sinful."—So honest a confession surprised as well as pleased his auditress, and doubtless it spoke well for the natural sincerity of the unfortunate recluse. Several nuns have, I am told, availed themselves of the permission now given, to quit their convents; alleging that they had been compelled to assume the veil; but such instances are still rare.

I remember having formerly told you in one of my letters, that I should abstain from mentioning *much* of what I heard relative to the clergy here, from a motive of delicacy, arising from my being myself of the protestant persuasion; and I assure you, I still adhere to my resolution, notwithstanding all which I have mentioned concerning them. It is a painful subject to the truly christian observer, whether he belong to one or the other church! Modes of worship, forms, and ceremonies, may differ in each, and purity of faith be preserved in one, more decidedly than in the other, but the grand features of true christianity are for ever *the same;* and I am sure both protestants and catholics of

I 2

116   CINTRA.

virtuous life and disposition, must be equally
shocked at the crimes to which I have
alluded!—Many of the Portugueze customs
are, as I have already said, very extraordinary, that is, they appear so to an English
person.

The women wear scarcely any petticoats,
even in winter, and some of the lower classes
none whatever, contenting themselves with
the chemise, covered only by the gown. The
latter never wear night-caps, and many still
continue the ancient fashion of sleeping in a
state of nature, considering clothes, during
the night, as equally unwholesome and unne-
cessary. Both sexes adopt this practice.
My informant, went one morning lately, to
visit a lady in Lisbon: upon entering the
room she (being still in bed,) invited her
visitor to sit down by her side, and arising
from her pillow embraced her; the latter
started involuntarily back, for the lady was
perfectly unclothed!—but this, I believe, does
not extend to the better educated and more
refined classes of society. The nobility (unlike those of Spain, who, in the days of Cervantes, left the custom to the common peo-

ple,) universally eat a great deal of garlic
and aniseed, and, in consequence, the
courtly whisper of the highest bred Fidalgo,
differs not at all from the coarse breath of
the meanest mechanic or peasant—it will be
easily imagined that neither resembled the
perfumed gale of Arabia!

Nothing can be more uncomfortable to a
stranger in Portugal, than the beds; their
extreme hardness really injures rather than
rests the bones (especially those of a *thin*
person). But the custom seems universal,
and it is impossible to obtain any relief,
unless you send to England for a hair mattress.
I have before mentioned, that beauty appears
rare among the inhabitants of Lisbon; and
that in families of high rank, it is still less
frequent. In the latter instance, this may be
easily explained, by the invariable custom,
among the Fidalgos, of marrying only with
the families of each other, and very frequently
of intermarrying with their near relations.
By these means they preserve the purity of
their blood, and perpetuate the defects of
their persons from generation to generation.

118   CINTRA.

One of the late kings of Portugal was united to his *aunt*, for the former reason.

The extreme familiarity of this people with their domestics strikes an English person at first sight in a forcible manner; and it is somewhat difficult to reconcile such a mode of conduct with their inherent arrogance of birth.   In the present state of society in England, a similar behaviour would be attended with considerable inconvenience; yet I certainly think, that even there, greater benevolence and kindness of manner between master and servant would be more consonant to the dictates of liberal policy, and true christianity.

Adieu.

LETTER XVI.

Cintra, August.

AFTER a fortnight of prolonged absence, upon official duties at Lisbon, Mr. B. is just returned to Cintra, and has, as well as myself, accompanied two gentlemen of his acquaintance in an interesting expedition, to pay a morning visit to the venerable *Principal* of Portugal, " Freire," at his retired quinta, a few miles distant from Cintra. We rode upon Bûrros,* and, setting off at ten o'clock in the morning, braved the rays of an almost vertical sun; but the latter was tempered by a strong breeze from the sea, and it was worth while to make *some* effort, in order to see so celebrated and so worthy a character. The road led us among the surrounding mountains, for the greater part of the way, from whence we had fine views of the romantic neighbourhood. Towards the end of our journey we re-entered the usual tawny disagreeable flat country, which incloses the more favoured valley of Cintra. As we rode along,

* Mules.

120   CINTRA.

the gentlemen gave us the outline of Freire's history.—He is " *Principal;*" a title of such high ecclesiastical dignity, as to be second only to that of " *Patriarch.*" The latter honour has been offered to him twice, by the king ; but he has constantly refused it, upon motives of the most noble simplicity. When the Revolution was first announced, his moral and religious character stood so high, that the Reformers considered his name as a tower of strength, and spared no exertions to obtain its sanction. Upon being solicited to join their party, and, after having declared boldly, that his oath to the king would for ever preclude him from taking any *active* part in the New Constitution, he added, that he would consent to give them the countenance of his temporary presence in their council, as he thought his extensive influence might be of service in restraining any acts of violence or crime. Nor did the good man overrate his persuasive powers, for he was so highly respected by *all parties,* as to be of essential use in the way he expected. Through his mild and equitable advice, the envious and secretly hostile feeling of the Portugueze towards the English, has been considerably checked; and I am told, that he admires our nation extremely. He strongly deprecated the absurd impolicy of quarrelling with us, and ably pointed out the various ways in which it would be in our power to crush the Portugueze, if needlessly provoked to so painful a trial of superiority. When the Cortes thought it necessary to their future plans to remove from their commands those British officers who had spent their blood, and employed their military knowledge in defence of Portugal, he did all in his power to oppose the measure, upon a principle of generous gratitude—but whether the latter advice was equally remarkable for *sound national policy*, may perhaps be a question: certain it is, that since native officers have been employed to command the army, much of its discipline, and consequently of its effective power, has already begun to fall off—what eventual results this circumstance may produce, time only can evince—on the other hand, Patriotic feeling seems to sanction the promotion of native commanders, in preference to foreigners however excellent

and honourable.   But this subject of course
does not fall within the province of women
to discuss with so much propriety as many
others—let us return to the amiable Principal.   Liberal and enlightened in his religious sentiments, he openly avowed his opinion
that the wealth and power of the superior
clergy was carried to a most improper height,
and upon learning that their revenues had
been reduced by the Cortes, one fourth
of their former amount, he said, " the latter
had been extremely temperate and moderate
in the decision," and that, " he himself had
expected the revenues would have been curtailed by the half.—And, for his own part,
he was perfectly satisfied with a reduced income."   What a striking (and I fear a *singular*) contrast does this apostolic conduct present, to the pride, bigotry, and rapacity of
many among his *dignified* brethren!—The
late unfortunate General Freire was his
relation, and he was described to us, as having
been an equally respectable and amiable character—some have thought him the *Russell*
of Portugal!   He died a martyr to the interests of his country, having expiated the

crime of patriotism upon the scaffold, about four years ago!—You may recollect, that, at that period, a desire to effectuate the deliverance of Portugal from the worse than Turkish despotism of the old government, first manifested itself in the north of the country; at Oporto more particularly, where the people are said to be superior, in moral feeling and sensibility, to those of Lisbon and its environs. They assimilate also much nearer to the English residents, in the neatness and industry of their habits. The town itself is cleaner and more commodious than Lisbon, and the race of inhabitants, generally considered, more worthy of being rescued from the trammels of ignorance and oppression. General Freire, was one of these patriots—every opprobious epithet it is possible to conceive, has been applied to his name, for he *failed* in his attempts; " Saviour, patriot, hero, guardian, God," are among the appellations of the present set of reformers, for they have *succeeded* in theirs! and yet they are inferior in *every way* to Freire. Thus, it frequently happens, that *circumstances* decide all; and the self same

124   CINTRA.

act which in adversity is *crime,* becomes in
prosperity, *virtue!* Having received all these
voluminous details, relative to the family con-
nections and the character of the Principal,
we could hardly fail in looking upon this
visit as an interesting event in our lives, and
were impatient to reach the retreat of so
much unassuming worth. We were fortunate in finding him at home, sitting in his
morning country dishabille, with another
visitor, whose equipage we had observed in
the court yard, as we entered. This was
one of his earliest acquaintance at the University of Coimbra, an ancient grey haired
bishop, whose name I have forgotten. The
latter was a thin spare figure, bent and
enfeebled by age, with a countenance wherein
I thought I could trace the mingled expressions of native benevolence, cautious observation, and a slight tinge of crafty policy;—
at first sight, and previous to our presenta-
tion, we should not have been aware of his
rank, as his dress was of the coarsest mate-
rials, consisting of a long flowing robe of
very shabby black cloth, soiled with dust,
ponderous boots and spurs, with a little skull

cap of greasy black silk, covering the bare
circle of his tonsured head; in his hand he
carried a taper ebony riding wand, tipped
with silver, and as tall as himself—and I
remarked upon his turning round, the solitary ornament of a pair of tarnished gold
tassels, which hung down upon his back.
The countenance of the Principal was singularly cheerful and benevolent.   I do not
think that an expression of *intellectual* superiority was strongly defined; but candour,
frankness, and good temper were written
upon his brow!   His person could not be
called dignified, being short, and heavy in
its proportions; but (as might readily be expected,) there were no signs of the over-
whelming rotundity and rubicond visage of
the jolly *Father Paul,* much less any indica-
tions of the proud and pampered prelate, to
be seen!   He received us with amiable and
hospitable courtesy, apologized to me (being
the only female of the party) for his rustic
dishabille, and showed us over the whole of
his house and gardens.   In the latter, we
drank from a sparkling fountain, a draught
of pure element, which he praised with as

much earnestness as if it had been nectar.
Nothing could be more simple and primitive
than the style of his table, and the furniture
of his apartments; the latter was comprized
in a few ancient wooden chairs and tables,
ranged along the bare white-washed walls;
the only decoration being two or three taudry
grottoes in glass cases, made of shells, foil
and rags—the handy-work of nuns; the
former was nearly as frugal as that of a hermit! The cloth had been laid in readiness
for his dinner; it was clean but coarse, the
plates of the commonest Delf ware, and the
spoons of plated metal, through which the
copper was abundantly visible; he offered
us some sweet wine, and made us taste the
only dish which was in a state of sufficient
forwardness to be produced from the adjoin-
ing kitchen.—It was a *national* one, composed
of rice boiled in milk, and strewed over with
powdered cinnamon and sugar. As we passed
through a gallery, looking down upon the
chapel, where he performs mass to the
surrounding peasantry, at a very early hour
every morning; we remarked a lamp burning before the altar, although the rays of a

bright meridian sun were streaming into the apartment: this custom is, I believe, universal in the catholic church, and reminded me of the ancient fires of Vesta, both having proceeded from the same original idea, and used, I believe, as the symbol of heavenly love. Here, the Principal rapidly dropt upon one knee, and made the sign of the cross upon his breast, without stopping for more than a second in the course of his lively and easy conversation. I cannot but confess, that this habitual reverence for holy places, (although in some instances it has degenerated into mere *outward* formality,) appeared to me in bright contrast to the careless indifference which many protestants are but too apt to display towards *their* altars and places of worship! For my own individual feelings, I find it impossible to enter *any* building devoted to the service of the Almighty, without a sensation of solemn and reverential awe, independent of the particular mode of worship which may happen to be celebrated there!

The gardens of this quinta were shaded by alleys of box, mingled with laurel, and

were evidently kept for purposes of use
rather than of ornament.   As we returned
to the house, I thought I had never before
seen so humble an episcopal residence!   It
was spacious, but constructed upon so plain
and unadorned a plan, that it at once resembled a country stable, and a prison; uniting
all the want of finish, the roughness, and
rusticity of the former, with the solidity and
gloom of the latter.   No train of domestics
in purple pomp, inhabited this modest retreat:
two grave looking servants in coarse black
dresses, alone attended, and his prime
favourite seemed to be a sleek tabby cat,
who was installed in one of the apartments.
We now left the Principal, charmed by his
manners, countenance, and habits of life; and
fully disposed to coincide in the opinion of
our conductors, that " Freire was decidedly
one of the first characters in Portugal."

LETTER XVII.

Cintra, August.
Victor Sassetti's Hotel.

WE have lately removed to this hotel, on account of several domestic annoyances which occurred at the former; and here we find still superior comfort and accommodation, together with a frank and attentive civility, which has nothing servile, but a great deal of kindness to recommend it; the air too, is cooler, from the circumstance of the house having been erected on higher ground than that of Senhor Costa (our first host). Victor (who is a native of Piedmont) deserves the greatest encouragement; his activity, industry, and good management, his liberality towards every guest, and to his own family and servants, are striking. His wife (a Portugueze) differs so much in all her habits from the usual run of her country-women, as to be the counterpart of her husband. They maintain her aged mother, a

VOL. I.   K

niece, and six fine children, (most of the latter are *beautiful*,) and live in the most united and affectionate manner. Since we came hither, the family of La C—— are arrived at Cintra, to pass the autumnal season. They have shown us much polite and hospitable attention, and altogether, I think them superior to any Portugueze family which I have yet seen. Their widowed mother, the Baroness de B., has the reputation of much worth and amiability; her manners are gentle and polished, in which respect I perceive that she is emulated by all her children. One of her daughters assured me that she has been so much liked and esteemed for her hospitality to strangers, as to have obtained from foreigners, by common consent, the title of " the lady of Portugal." I was sorry for my own sake to find that she speaks only her native language; but the rest of the family converse fluently in French. I employ myself in drawing a good deal; the costumes of the peasantry, and the lovely scenery of Cintra afford ample scope to the pencil; but the climate does *not* agree with me, the heat and the dampness of the air are both too relaxing, and in my case have induced a degree of physical languor, which is but too apt to increase mental anxiety and depression; nor am I the only foreigner who has found the same effect from a continued residence at Cintra, all beauteous as it is.

I ascended the mountains, a few days since, to witness the ceremony of what is called " a church feast," held in the convent of " Nossa Senhora da Pênha" (our Lady of the Rock), upon the topmost peak of one of the highest. There I witnessed a great deal of what I must call " mummery," and heard some bad music; a few scripture characters (represented by children dressed up for the purpose) occasionally mingled in the service, and there was a shrill chorus of *cherubim*, which was any thing but *angelic;* the latter small personages were decked in the most taudry grotesque costume that can be imagined, and covered with foil and dirty ostrich feathers, altogether reminding me strongly of the glories of a London chimney-sweeper on May-day.

132   CINTRA.

LETTER XVIII.

Cintra, Sept. 21st.

Since I dispatched my last letter to you, we
have seen a good deal of Portugueze society, chiefly at the house of the Baroness
de B. From having opened their house for
so many years past, to English and foreign
visitors, some of whom have been of the
first families, and of distinguished merit and
talent, they have risen wonderfully above the
singular prejudices of their age and nation.
The young Donnas frequently express to us
how much they regret the neglected state of
education, which (with a few exceptions)
is prevalent among the Portugueze families of all ranks. They have even lamented what they termed their own deficiency in
this respect; but if such *really* exists, I am
sure it is very difficult to be discovered, and
admirably supplied by their native talent and
tact. How many soi-disant accomplished

young ladies have I seen, in England, who are unworthy of the least comparison, and yet the most extravagant expense of money, time, and patience, has been lavished upon their education! The eldest of the La C.'s is small, low in stature, and very dark complexioned: her hands and feet beautifully slender and delicate; indeed, almost all the Portugueze ladies have small feet, though not generally so *well formed* as those of the Spanish, nor are they reported to walk so well as the latter, to whom, I believe, the celebrated " *Foot of fire* " must by *all* women be conceded. Without being handsome, she has an ingenuous sensible countenance, where it is not difficult to trace a degree of sensibility, which she said herself, was sometimes too great for her happiness. I think I never heard a finer voice—it is powerful at times, when she is in good health and spirits, and always sweet, while her taste and brilliancy of execution are of a high order of excellence. She wished, the other day, at her own house, to give me some idea of a *trio* in the opera of La Fille de l'Air, mentioned by Madame de Stael in her Corinne, but having no piano

forte at Cintra, what was to be done? In
this dilemma, her brother and his friend, two
young officers, came to her assistance.
They supported the under vocal parts of the
trio, and in addition, gave a correct and very
pleasing *imitation* of the violin and bassoon
accompaniment. The effect was excellent.
Sen. I. (her brother) has a fine rich bass
voice, and sung the buffo part with considerable expression. *Not one of the party* can
read music, and Donna C. herself, with the
exception of a very few lessons which she received formerly from an Italian master, is
wholly the pupil of nature. Her vocal memory is perfectly astonishing; and in this point
she is nearly equalled by her two sisters, who
sing a little, but do not possess the distinguished voice of the elder. The second
daughter has a speaking eye—full of animation! I should think that she had *quicker* abi-
lities, perhaps, than any of the family, and she
has great variety and brilliancy in her conversation, without being less feeling and graceful
in her manners. The youngest is so small,
that she resembles a sylph or a fairy; she
appears gentle and amiable, is fond of oc-

cupation, and I generally find her bending over a frame, where she embroiders like a second Arachne! The baroness sees company every evening: Corcundas and Constitutionalists are equally admitted. I have never gone in, that I have not met a large party assembled, conversing as they walked up and down the long drawing room, or playing at cards. The latter forms the chief occupation of most Portugueze families, the card tables being set the moment breakfast is over;—indeed, like Boniface with his ale, they seem to

" Eat, drink, and sleep upon their cards."

It is *very* rarely that one sees a room furnished with *books;* but this ought not to excite surprise in a country which has produced but one great author, and where foreign literature, until lately, has been prohibited, as dangerous alike to church and state. I have been assured, upon very good authority however, that this forbidden fruit has been *secretly* plucked, with greedy eagerness, in spite of the dragons who guarded it; and,

136   CINTRA.

what is singular, by the dragons themselves,
who are reported to be particularly delighted with Voltaire, Diderot, &c. &c. and to
collect their works, and others of an infidel
tendency, for their private delectation. Indeed the growth of atheistical and deistical
principles is said to be of alarming rapidity,
both among the laity and the clergy in this
country. I hope such an assertion is not
true, but I could not be *surprised* were it
really the case; the unbecoming intoler-
ance of the Romish tenets, if they fail of
engendering the most complete bigotry, *naturally* tend to the production of the opposite
extreme ! In countries where the liberty of
free discussion upon religious subjects is
allowed, mere *doubts* are not so fatally dangerous : a spirit of inquiry, of investigation,
is thereby excited, which, if fairly conducted,
is the best and surest friend to Christianity.
It has always been a great pleasure to me to
recollect, that one of the brightest ornaments
of the Romish church, and the model for
all churchmen, of whatever persuasion, the
immortal Fenelon, was by no means what is
termed an *orthodox* Catholic.

CINTRA. **137**

I have just received a visit from the Spanish ambassador extraordinary, and his countess. I dare not attempt to *spell* their names, the guttural sound of which renders the task hopeless to a foreigner. The Ambassador is a dignified and graceful personage, and the ambassadress a pretty and engaging woman, whose complexion is as fair and delicate as that of any English beauty, while the latter can seldom boast of such dark and richly fringed hazel eyes. Like most Spanish women, she is full of fire and animation; talks French fluently, and is wholly free from hauteur or affectation. I do not hear that she possesses an *appendage* which is but too common to the ladies of her country—" the *cicesbeo*." There appears to be a great (or rather a *little*) jealousy generally existing in the minds of the Portugueze towards Spaniards; the women, especially, seem to hate each other cordially; and if I were to give implicit credence to all the tales I have been told by the former of the latter, my hair (being a sober English woman) might chance to stand an end! I must, in candour, acknowledge, that I thought the

138   CINTRA.

ladies of Lisbon behaved, generally speaking, with great neglect towards the ambassadress, in suffering her to remain for nearly the
whole of her sojourn among them, in her
solitary hotel, without paying her the attention even of a ceremonious visit.   There
was a want of hospitality and of kind feeling
about this mode of conduct, which appeared
the more glaring, as it was well known that
her family was not only one of the highest
in Spain, but that she had received a remarkably good education, and possessed
personal claims to esteem and respect.

Among many anecdotes of Spanish customs and manners, I will repeat the following, which will, doubtless, somewhat surprise
you.—The late Baron de B. (a Portugueze,)
was travelling, some years since, in Spain,
and passed a few days under the roof of a
lady of high rank, whose husband was one
of the most distinguished persons in the
government.   The bed-rooms there are
frequently without doors, a slight curtain
only covering the entrance to each.   The
baron was a favourite of the fair hostess.
One morning, as she was in her own apart-

ment, she heard his footsteps passing along
the gallery, and called out to him to come
and sit down. The gentleman hesitated a
good deal, surprised at her freedom of manner, (for the Portugueze are far more
reserved than the Spaniards in every
outward appearance,) and perceiving her
maid standing at the entrance, he asked, if
her lady was dressed and would admit him?
" Dressed!" repeated the laughing damsel,
"what difference can that make? come in—
come in." He accordingly complied, and
found her in bed, with one foot exposed to
the inspection of the family surgeon, who was
preparing a penknife to cut her excellency's
corns! A French belle receives male visitants at her toilette, but she has too much
coquetry to exhibit a *disagreeable* spectacle
to the eyes of her flatterers: how impolitic
the sang-froid of the other was I need
not waste time in expressing. The same
lady had a very large party of distinguished
nobility at dinner. She intended to go
to the theatre at night, and a few minutes before the proper hour, her maid entered the apartment, with a box of jewels,

140   CINTRA.

from which she coolly selected what she
thought most splendid, and putting them
upon her mistress, chattered the whole time
to the noble visitants, without appearing in
the least restrained or impressed by their
superior rank. As soon as her excellency
was adorned, she called for coffee, and
placing her feet upon a pan of hot charcoal,
(used during the winter, in Spain,) she carelessly turned one beautiful leg over the
other, so as to display not only their own
symmetry, but a pair of very rich garters,
which hung down in golden tassels, and began to *smoke.*

The Portugueze ambassadress had at
that time just arrived in Spain. She en-
quired what would be expected of her, from
the Hidalgos, among whom she was come to
reside; and was told, that it might be proper
to begin by giving a ball and supper. Accordingly, the tickets of invitation were issued,
and a magnificent entertainment prepared.
The stated night arrived, and the Portugueze
covered with jewels, prepared to receive her
guests; but to her great surprise, scarcely
any one appeared! Hour after hour elapsed,

and still the musicians played to the walls and benches! The supper was equally neglected, and in short the whole entertainment thrown away. A few days afterwards, she received from the French ambassadress, a solution of the mystery. " How did your excellency word the tickets of invitation?"— " I scarcely understand your question." " I mean, *who* did you mention in each card?" " The heads, and the principal members of every family, of course." "No one else?" " Certainly not ; *who* should there have been in addition?" At these words the French woman yielded to an inexpressible burst of laughter. " Forgive me, Madam," said she, " but your simplicity is so infinitely amusing! you should never have asked husband and wife together; had you invited every lady and her *cicesbeo*, your rooms would have overflowed!" The Portugueze, in order to prove the truth of this hint, gave another ball, wording her invitations in the *proper* manner, and the consequence was, that her entertainment was the most brilliant and numerously attended that it is possible to conceive.

LETTER XIX.

Cintra, September 28th.

I MET an interesting couple this morning
in my walk. Passing through the shady
lane which leads from hence to the Marialva, I perceived a young soldier seated
upon the stone bench by the road side, with
one of the prettiest peasant girls I had ever
seen; they appeared heated and fatigued,
yet were chattering and laughing with much
cheerfulness over a large water-melon, which
the man was cutting, and of which he had
just given her a share as I came up to
them. I have hardly ever beheld a finer
couple! Stopping to observe the beauty of
the girl more nearly, I pretended to admire the glass buttons which ornamented
her jacket; upon which, she pointed to a
gold cross which I wore, and made me com-
prehend that she also admired *my* taste in

decoration. The soldier, in the mean time, had cut another slice of the refreshing fruit, and offered it to my acceptance, with a respectful good will, which was really graceful. I asked if the young person was his wife? To which he replied in broken English, with great animation, "Yes, minha Senhora, she my wife; *much good for me !*" I could not forbear (and wherefore should I have forborne?) gratifying him by saying, as I took my leave, "She is very pretty!" and I heard him telling her, after I had passed on, that I meant " muita bonita," which seemed to make her laugh heartily. I never saw more ingenuous countenances than those of both these rustics, and I am determined, from the innocent expression of her lovely features, to believe, that she was indeed a wife. Those persons who form their ideas of beauty from mere *red and white,* would not perhaps have admired her style; and those who have never seen Spanish or Portugueze eyes, may talk as much as they please of the charms of blue or grey orbs; nay the very ancients may rave about their eyes of Venus, which I

144   CINTRA.

believe they asserted to be of an indefinite
colour, wavering between violet and brown;
but certain I am, that all such *must* " *pale
their ineffectual fire,*" if placed in comparison
with these *sable* diamonds, these living stars!
The expression of feeling, particularly that
of gratitude, seems to be very energetic
among the Portugueze peasantry, and it has
happened several times, that I myself have
had occasion to witness it.   I merely gave a
trifle, to an aged woman here, for the relief
of her orphan grand-children; some time
afterwards, when I was quitting the hotel,
she rushed into my room, threw herself at
my feet, and embraced my knees with the
tears running down her cheeks.   " God
bless you! I am much obliged by your
kindness," was all she could utter; and I
am convinced that it was not the money so
much, as our having shown an interest in
the fate of her orphans, which affected her
so sensibly!

   At another time, a woman who sold goat's
milk to us every morning, had received some
affront from a drunken fellow, half an idiot,
who belonged to the hotel. I pitied her

agitation, and sent to desire her to come up
stairs, wishing, if I must acknowledge the
whole truth, to have a nearer view of her
costume, and Moorish physiognomy.   She
accordingly entered the room, making repeated motions with her head and arms,
much resembling the eastern *salam*, and
falling upon her knees, clung about me,
while she related the story of her quarrel,
accompanying the narration with floods of
tears.   I never saw a more singular figure,
her skin, independent of its native swarthy
hue, was blackened by the scorching influence of the sun, to the complexion of an
Egyptian mummy; her lean form resembled
that of a skeleton, her waist was of an
enormous length, and as slender in its proportions as that of a wasp; the veins and
sinews started in ghastly relief from her throat
and arms, and her dark eyes, drowned in
tears, sunk deep in their bony sockets; a
coarse scarlet cloth petticoat with a broad
blue border, and a coloured linen jacket,
an uncoifed grizzled shaggy head, and thick
high-heeled leather boots, resembling those

146   CINTRA.

worn by men, formed her costume; altogether, she was an object which having once
seen, it would, I think, be difficult to forget!

Nothing more excites our surprize, than
the indifference which the generality of
persons in the higher classes evince towards
the beauty, the verdure, the shade, and the
coolness of Cintra! They seem to prefer
the disgusting streets of Lisbon and its
environs, to these striking scenes of natural
loveliness and simplicity; almost every quinta
we see here, is suffered to run to ruin; and
some houses, which belong to the nobility,
are in só dilapidated a state as to be nearly
unfit to afford shelter from the weather!
Indeed we are told by many Portugueze,
(who did not seem to feel they were exhibit-
ing any proof of vitiated taste,) that Cintra
was by no means a favourite residence, even
among those families who had property
there.   It forms to Lisbon, what Richmond
is to London; and is chiefly frequented
during the Summer months, by flocks of
citizens, who come down to the hotels, on
the Saturday night, and leave it again for
Lisbon, on the Monday following; passing

CINTRA. **147**

the interval, in riding (often at full speed in a riotous and brutal manner,) the poor burros, which are let out for hire, in gormandizing and in gambling. Adieu.

———

L 2

LETTER XX.

Cintra, October 4th.

WE frequently meet in society here, a certain hero of romance, of whom I formerly spoke, as the proprietor of the pretty quinta of the fountain; I now find, that there are two ways of telling his story; while the gentle lovers of the *novel*, insist upon it, that this youthful "stranger," who lives thus separated for his *adored* but faithless wife, brooding in secret over feelings of mingled severity and tenderness, and lost to the enjoyments of the gay world, is deserving of the utmost commiseration, his enemies assert, that his own unfeeling indifference to her happiness and reputation, aided by his supine acquiescence in the opinions of an austere tutor who resides with him, and has ever shown a most unwarrantable dislike to the lady in question, have been the only causes of the separation of the parties. The presumptuous interference of the tutor, is even said

to have extended to the regulation of her
wardrobe, (a piece of officiousness which no
woman could be expected to forgive,) and
this from motives of a pecuniary nature,
which it is broadly hinted, turned more upon
his own eventual benefit, than upon that of
his patron and pupil; as far as *I* have been
able to judge, no person ever had less the
appearance of suffering from mental uneasiness than the young gentleman in question;
he enters into society as willingly as any
body else, has a round dimpled face (untouched by a single line of " carking care,")
and the air of a careless schoolboy, rather
than of a sentimental sufferer.   An old
gentleman of the neighbourhood, rich and
independent, and consequently not much
afraid of " speaking his mind" (as the phrase
is,) upon all occasions, told me very lately,
that the young senhor had called upon him
twice since his arrival at Cintra, but had not
been admitted; a thing which is very rare
in Portugal, where the custom of saying
" not at home" is rarely practised, and far
less properly understood.   " I have called
at your door several times, Mr. B——" said

150   CINTRA.

he, " but you did not let me in!"   " Pray
senhor," returned the old gentleman in his
driest manner, " have you released your
wife from her imprisonment?"   " No sir!"
—" Very well, when you let *her out*, I will
let *you in*; and not before."—Upon which
they parted in mutual indignation!

The Portugueze, both in the higher and
lower classes, are superstitiously prone to a
belief in omens, lucky and unlucky days,
divination by cards, religious miracles, &c.
&c. although every idea of the possibility
of the re-appearance of departed spirits,
seems generally scoffed at and denied. The
tone of their minds is rarely high and
intellectual, and therefore the gross and
puerile nature of their superstitions ought
not to create surprise.

A lady here told my fortune by the cards,
in a very interesting lively manner, and had
talent enough to fix my attention in spite of
good sense; she mentioned that the Polanders are universally addicted to the oracles
of cards and dice, and are almost all *fatal-
ists*, even in their more serious opinions.   A
gentleman of that nation, who was formerly

in the habit of visiting at her house, once undertook to predict the fortune of one of her female relations by means of dice; he threw them in a particular way, with many strange ceremonies, and then remarked, that such and such occurrences would happen to her, in such and such a time. He was extremely ridiculed, as what he had foretold came scarcely within the bounds of possibility, much less of *probability;* but the subsequent events faithfully verified his words; as there are some distinguished names both in England and Portugal mixed up in the above relation, I am not at liberty to mention the particulars, but at all events, I must say, that the Polander, if he was not actually an adept in the *occult* sciences, had at least a very keen and extended vision with respect to possible *political* events; the fate of the lady depended much upon affairs connected with the Portugueze and English governments, and it appears to me not improbable that this *wise-man's* mind foreboded the changes which have so lately taken place in the former, although they were *then* at a great distance. This is the only *rationale* of the circumstances which I can devise, and, even with this assistance, I confess the talent of the Polander must have been *very extraordinary*, and bears a considerable resemblance to that of the Russian officer, mentioned in the "Memoirs of the Margravine of Bareith," by Thibault, who predicted, in so strange and minute a manner, the various events in the life of that princess, who was then a child. Perhaps I shall have tired you with this long dissertation, and I believe it might as well have been omitted altogether, since I am restrained from mentioning it in that *detailed* manner which would have enabled you to take an interest in it, by the opportunity it afforded you of *judging for yourself*. Among other superstitions to which the Polish nation is addicted, I may be forgiven for relating the following, as its elegance of fancy, almost redeems its absurdity. Every individual is supposed to be born under the influence of some particular destiny or fate, which it is impossible for him to avoid. The month of his nativity has a mysterious connection with one of the known precious stones, and when a person wishes to make the object of his affections an acceptable present, a *ring* is invariably given, composed of the jewel by which the fate of that object is imagined to be determined and described.   For instance, a woman is born in January; her ring must therefore be a jacynth or a garnet, for these stones belong to that peculiar month of the year, and express " constancy and fidelity."   I saw a list of them all, which the Polander gave to the lady in question, and she has allowed me to copy it.—viz.

" *January* — Jacynth or garnet. — Constancy and fidelity in every engagement.

" *February* — Amethyst. — This month and stone preserves mortals from strong passions, and ensures them peace of mind.

" *March* — Bloodstone. — Courage, and success in dangers and hazardous enterprises.

" *April*—Sapphire or diamond.—Repentance, and innocence.

" *May*—Emerald.—Success in love.

" *June*—Agate.—Long life and health.

" *July*—Cornelian or ruby.—The forget-

154   **CINTRA.**

fulness or the cure of evils springing from friendship or love.

" *August*—Sardonyx.—Conjugal fidelity.

" *September* — Chrysolite. — Preserves from, or cures folly.

" *October*—Acquamarine, or opal.—Misfortune and hope.

" *November*—Topaz.—Fidelity in friendship.

" *December*—Turquoise, or malakite.— The most brilliant success and happiness in every circumstance of life; the turquoize has also the property of securing friendly regard; hence the old saying, that 'he who possesses a turquoise will always be sure of friends.' "

LETTER XXI.

Cintra, October 4th.

I WENT last night, (taking advantage of Mr. B.'s return for one day only,) to the mountain upon the extreme summit of which, are the remains of the Castello dos Mouros; (moorish castle.) The view of the surrounding country, as we climbed the steep ascent, was beautiful. The Penha convent, on the twin mountain's top, had a particularly fine effect; its grey walls and the foundation rocks were bathed in a flood of purple glory, a farewell favour from the departing sun! Seen in this point of view, they seemed to me representative of the Romish religion; *both* lose, when closely examined by the cool and sober light of truth, and *both* have the property of dazzling the eyes, and of charming the senses, when clothed in the unreal splendours lent by a heated imagination. We were not able fully to satisfy

156   CINTRA.

our curiosity: as being encumbered by the
presence of our little boy, we did not find
it safe to climb the steepest aclivity, upon
which the castle stands.

I walked again this morning to the beautiful
quinta of the fountain, indulging in no un-
pleasing reverie as I listened to the usual soft
fall of the water, and to the soothing murmur
of the wood pigeons, which, as I have before
told you, build among these chestnut shades.
I have often heard it said, that a person who
resides amid the scenery of the Cumberland and Westmorland lakes must infallibly
become in some degree a poet, or else be
a decided fool; that is to say, he must either
be wholly enchanted, or stupidly insensible,
there being no medium.   I could almost
have held the same opinion in regard to
this romantic quinta, had I not been aware
of a scene which took place there the other
day, at ten o'clock in the morning, in which
so many individuals were engaged, that it
would be rather too sweeping a censure, to
pronounce that they were *all* as much blocks
as the rocks which surounded them!   Two
large card-tables were placed, one on each

Drawn by M. Baillie.

PORTUGUEZE SCENERY & PEASANTS.

Published, June, 1824, by John Murray, London.

side of the lovely fountain, round which above thirty persons were seated, playing at rondo, a gambling game, at which the Portugueze often lose enormous sums. This day, the place was once more silent and solitary, the pure ear of the nymph of the Spring was no longer shocked by the sound of vulgar and incongruous revelry; yet, from the apartments of the house to which the quinta belonged, there rose upon the air, at intervals, the shouts and exclamations of a party, (higher in their rank, yet, I suspect, little more refined or intellectual in their pleasures,) mingled with the strokes of the mace, and the clashing of the balls of a billiard table; methought, at every blow, I beheld the trembling dryads shrinking deeper into their verdant retreats! However, I ought not to be too severe in my censure; in Portugal there are so few mental resources to engage or fertilize the mind, that a man whose time is unoccupied by the daily routine of a business or profession, (or, as is *now* frequently the case, by schemes of *political* intrigue,) must be wholly and listlessly idle, if he has not recourse to these

158   CINTRA.

sort of amusements: besides, there is *now*
a possibility, that the taste for such frivolous
employment of time may decline, and a wish
for the attainment of knowledge increase,
together with the means of its acquirement.
The gates are at length beginning to open
for the admission of foreign literature; slowly
and sullenly indeed, groaning and creak-
ing as they turn, and still impeded in their
progress by remaining superstitions and
political jealousies; but still they *are* opening, and I trust they will soon find many a
ready hand stretched forth, to pour oil upon
their hinges.   I heard lately, and from good
authority, that it was already in contempla-
tion to publish a literary journal, and that
the Edinburgh and Quarterly Reviews had
been sent for, as models for the Portugueze
tyros; but the New Monthly Magazine
which has recently started into just and distinguished notice in our own country, and
which has been met with open arms in America, would, I think, be a more eligible pattern; as it treats of more light and general
subjects than either of the former Reviews,
whose abstruse disquisitions upon science

are *at present* much beyond the reach of
Portugueze critics! This dawn of light
has doubtless sprung from the effects of the
constitutional form of government, the original
promoters of which ought not to be denied
their due share of credit for that and other
beneficial efforts. Yet, is this *good* most
strangely mingled with *evil;* for although
the present ruling power is more liberal in
some points than the former, it is equally
ignorant and arrogant in others: indeed it
appears to us to be quite as *despotic* in its
way, and is only worthy to be considered as
the lesser plague of the two; when we consider some of its late proceedings, evincing
as much absurdity of judgment, as a want
of faith and integrity, it is impossible to feel
either a respect for its character, or any
strong persuasion of its duration. A
succession of tyrannical idiots, unhappily
invested with despotic power, have for many
ages ruled this wretched land; last year it
pleased the fates, that they should be suddenly overthrown; but who are those who
now grasp the reins of the state? a band of
firm, upright, benevolent and enlightened

160   CINTRA.

patriots?—Far, far from it!—The possession of unaccustomed authority has already
begun to turn their heads; they

> " Assume the God,
> Affect to nod,
> And *think* they shake the spheres."

It is more than probable, and certainly
little to be regretted, that, ere long, they
will bring down upon themselves a severe
lesson; but whatever may occur, all good
men are bound to hope, that the former
Turkish system of government will never again
be tolerated; there are many who would
be mad and criminal enough to attempt its
revival, but the spirit of the age, (so clearly
and universally demonstrated,) would, I think,
prove an effectual bar to their selfish project!
The people *at large* are surely worth saving
and teaching; nor is it likely that the stream
of knowledge, having once been set at liberty,
(even though it may have been effectuated
by unworthy hands,) will ever again be pent
up in the former narrow channel! Long
may it continue to flow, gaining force as it
goes, overcoming every obstacle, opening

new ways amid the arid deserts of ignorance and superstition, proceeding "from strength to strength," still, like the Nile, fertilizing, cheering and blessing the soil over which it rolls, until it at length expands into a clear, pure, and widely diffusive flood, which will wash away all traces of past error and crime, and render the name of Portugal distinguished and honourable among the nations of the world!

A very pretty anecdote of a child of Victor's has this moment come to my knowledge, and it will refresh your mind as well as my own, if I relate it to you, rather than dwell any longer upon such high and mighty topics! Mr. Baillie had given the boy (who is about eleven years of age, very handsome, and engaging in his manners,) a nuovo cruzado, to spend at a fair here, which took place nearly a month since; the little fellow, however, had kept it unbroken, until now, when he has purchased with it a very pretty English shawl for his mother: I really envied her feelings upon receiving so unequivocal a token of affection and generosity. Adieu.

VOL. I.   M

162   CINTRA.

LETTER XXII.

Cintra, Oct. 7th.

WE have made another and more successful attempt to reach the summit of the
mountain upon which the Castello dos Mouros
is built, and were gratified by the finest bird's-
eye prospect of the country that we had yet
seen. We were shown the Moorish fountain
of the purest and most transparent water possible, of which we had previously heard much,
and I had imagined more, fancying it to be situated at the extreme summit of the mountain, open to the purifying influence of the
free winds of heaven, where the moon
and stars nightly gazed upon the reflection
of their glorious beauty, and the morning
beheld her blushes given back again in
softened loveliness ! These fine expectations
soon vanished when I beheld the reality,
and I found, to my disappointment, that the
celebrated Moorish fountain was nothing
more romantic than a common cold bath,

built beneath the remaining arches of a
dismal stone vault, dark, damp, and deep,
the first view of which quenched, effectually, all my *poetical* ideas. The castle itself covers a vast extent of irregular
ground, and must indeed have been a superb
and haughty fastness, almost impregnable,
both from strength and locality. The chapel is nearly entire, and there are considerable remains of the different apartments and
staircases—some of the former have three
walls, built by human industry, and the
fourth formed of the solid rock. Rosemary,
thyme, marjoram, chamomile, &c. &c. grow
in great profusion among these wild crags,
and the air is delightfully perfumed with
their aromatic odour. The change of tem-
perature from the late intolerable and ener-
vating heat of summer, to the present autumnal freshness, is a perfect medicine to
myself and child. We can now walk even in
the middle of the day among the rocks,
gaining health and strength at every step.
The air is purer, and more bracing than
lower down in the valley, or in the close
woods, and the elevation is not sufficient

164   CINTRA.

to render it sharp or rarefied. These
mountains, in fact, are not by any means *lofty*,
and when compared with those in Switzerland, appear like mere pigmies. They do
not consist of one prodigious and connected
surface, but are broken into a thousand irregular masses, (some of which are very
small,) as if they had been heaped one upon
the other in consequence of an earthquake,
or by the force of a rapid torrent; and yet,
there is no appearance of a stream among
them at present; no sparkling brook—no
graceful cascade, nor miniature lake, not even
one of those narrow falls of water, resembling
a line of liquid silver, which are so common in
other mountainous regions. The grand
aqueduct has, I believe, effectually drained
every source of this beautiful and precious
element, which is carried along the heights,
and descends into the reservoir by means of
small tunnels formed of red tile, and protect-
ed from the impurities it might collect in its
progress by a rude covering of cemented lime
and sand. This superb work of art, from which
the whole city of Lisbon is supplied with
water, was erected by order of that celebrated

statesman, the Marquis de Pombal, answering a double end—that of benefiting the inhabitants, and that of plausibly employing for many months a large standing army, which he (for political reasons) was afraid of disbanding, although he was under a promise of doing so at the termination of a war.

The Portugueze (like most foreigners who have fallen under my observation) eat a great variety at their meals, and it may be added, a great quantity also! They generally breakfast upon very substantial fare; coffee and tea forming only the accompaniments to hot beef steaks, fish, &c. Their dinner, which takes place in the middle of the day, is comparatively slight, and irregularly served. Those very few families who happen to approve the customs of the English, take tea in the evening, but it is more common to omit this refreshment altogether. Every body eats supper, which is, in fact, the principal meal of the day, and here an old Fidalga of my acquaintance is said to evince, that, in spite of her advanced age, she possesses the digestion of an ostrich! The favorite dish at breakfast of a young donna, by her own confession,

166   CINTRA.

would somewhat astonish the fastidious delicacy of *our* fine ladies, or of Lord Ogleby,
of famous memory, whose chief objection to
the worthy citizen, his host, consisted in his
liking to eat,

     " Vulgar fellow ! hot rolls and butter in July !"

I cannot, however, believe that her taste is
not peculiar to herself alone.   The dish is
as follows, and it forms a totally new article, I
should imagine, in the gastronomic calendar.
" A large thick slice of hot leavened bread,
strewed with salt and pepper, soaked in vi-
negar, seasoned highly with garlic, and
swimming in that filthy sort of oil, which I
believe I once before mentioned as preferred
here to all others, being of so rank a scent as
well as flavour, that it is impossible not to
perceive *its effects* for many hours after it has
been eaten, in the taint it leaves upon the
breath."   There is a species of cake, composed of this oil, honey, and fine flower, of
which the best families are extravagantly fond,
and which they introduce upon every occasion.   I always fancy I can smell it, at the

distance of several yards.   The constant
and profuse use of oil in their food, joined to
the relaxing effects of indolence and of climate, may probably be the cause of the almost universal weakness of digestion, and
want of personal strength, so common among
the inhabitants of Lisbon.   The peasantry
appear to enjoy far better health; perpetual
exercise under the influence of summer's
sun and winter's wind, hardens their muscles
and reduces their flesh: their food, also, is
remarkably spare, and by no means of a fat-
tening nature,—dried fish, coarse black
looking bread, made of barley or Indian
corn, with a head or two of garlic, and sometimes goats'-milk cheese, dry, salt, and nearly impenetrable to the teeth, resembling that
upon which the goatherds regaled Don
Quixote amid the cork tree mountains.
They often live to an advanced age, more
particularly at Cintra; but this used, I am
told, to be the case formerly more than at
present, for of late, the number of sudden
deaths among persons in the prime of life
has increased to an alarming degree.   Convulsions, palsy, and apoplexy, are very fre-

168   CINTRA.

quent, particularly among the middling and higher classes. Sometimes whole families inherit these dreadful diseases; and one young lady with whom I am acquainted, is perpetually liable to the former, during the hot months of the year. She is of a delicate frame and very nervous. If she is overfatigued, or agitated by any unpleasant emotion, convulsive spasms immediately come on; and for the first few days after the recent death of her father, she was repeatedly attacked in this manner, and so violently, that her life was thought to have been in danger. The mention of his decease reminds me of a barbarous custom in Portugal, which yet remains to be abolished. Immediately upon the death of any member of a family, the rest are obliged, beginning from that day, to receive, in formal ceremony, the visit of every person of their acquaintance, who, hastily assuming a black dress, run in crowds to pay their set compliments of condolence. The surviving, and sometimes deeply afflicted relatives, range themselves upon a sofa at the upper end of the room, where they are obliged to sit in state, for the first eight

days after the death, exposed to the gaze of
hard-hearted or careless curiosity.   When
the corpse is to be buried, the heir of the deceased takes charge of the key of the coffin,
and is obliged to unlock the lid, when the
body remains with the face uncovered during the whole of the funeral service.   They
always bury in churches, to the great scandal
of every person of sane mind and benevolent
regard for the health of the living; and the
unwholesome effects of this practice have
arisen to such a height, that it has lately
been laid before the consideration of the
Cortes.   Quick lime is often poured into the
vaults in order to obviate the evil, but feeling and delicacy are offended by this method.
Certain it is, that to the freed spirit, nothing
can be of less importance than the manner
in which the gross mortal husk is disposed of.
The body is like a garment, which, when it is
worn out or destroyed, may either be cast into
a lumber chest, or thrown wholly away, it
matters not which to the late wearer ! Yet,
to the fond and weeping survivors, the idea
of any thing approaching to disrespect, is

170   CINTRA.

often insupportably distressing; and for this
reason, surely, a certain decency and tenderness ought always to be preserved in the
manner of treating the bodies of the departed.

LETTER XXIII.

Cintra, Oct.

A FEW weeks since, an assassination of an officer took place in the streets of Lisbon: it is the first which has come to our knowledge since our arrival in the country, and is talked of as rather an uncommon circumstance at *this time of the year*, for it is chiefly during the dark nights of winter that such occurrences are frequent. There has been for the last few days a grand church feast, held at Mafra, a celebrated edifice about twelve miles from hence, being at once a palace, a church, and a convent. A great deal of company attended this ceremony, among them the king, queen, and royal family, who appear to have a singular taste in their *amusements*. It may very well be said of them, as the ancient French historians said of the English nation, that " ils se divertissent moult tristement!" The king in particular has never quitted home since

172   CINTRA.

he returned, but to say prayers to the
different virgins, at one or other of the
neighbouring churches or convents! No
country under heaven abounds more with
the *outward* signs of devotion than Portugal.
The virgin stands godmother to almost all
the females, and most of the streets of the
city are named in honour of persons or
places celebrated in scripture or church history.   Donna Maria de Luz, (our lady of
light,) I have already mentioned; her aunts
are Donna Maria de Picdade, and Donna
Maria Madre de Deos; and her cousin (a
very amiable and estimable person) is called
Donna Maria de Carmo.   The house in
which the La C. family reside, near Lisbon,
is named "Calvario;" we ourselves are
lodged in the "Rua San Domingos," and
shortly intend to take a house in the "Pateo
das Chagas," (i. e. the place of the five
wounds of Christ).   A fine church, built by
the late queen, has a still more extraordinary distinction, being called after, and dedicated to the *heart of Jesus* ("Coracao do
Jesus."). I believe that I have already mentioned the latter to you. The king has some

idea of residing in future at the palace of
the Ajuda. I lately saw both himself and
two of the princesses, his daughters, in the
ancient palace at Cintra, during a visit of a
few hours which they made to that melancholy pile. His countenance was by no
means prepossessing; his features irregular,
and he had every appearance of being
frightened to death. He received but a
cold reception from the peasantry, which I
rather wondered to observe, as they have
hitherto had the reputation of extraordinary
loyalty, and to the house of Braganza in
particular. The two princesses (one of them
a widow, having been married to the late infant of Spain,) were mild and pleasing in
their appearance and demeanour. The
queen I have not yet seen; she is reported
to be growing extremely *devout*. The chief
things worthy of notice in this palace are,
the apartment in which Don Alfonzo, a former king, was confined for many years, the
victim of fraternal cruelty; and where the
prints of his daily footsteps are still plainly
visible; and the chair in which the celebrated Sebastian sat, at the last council of state

174   CINTRA.

he ever held, only a few days previous to his
mysterious disappearance.   The architecture is Moorish, and there are one or two
halls of audience which are not inelegant.

The marriages in this country, among the
upper classes, are arranged in a most absurd
and unfortunate manner.   The ceremonies
connected with them are endless, and attended with such enormous expense, that
frequently the young couple are under the
necessity of living in real poverty for several
years, in consequence of their foolish and im-
provident ostentation upon the day of their
nuptials.   Every husband, however narrow
his circumstances, is obliged to furnish his
wife with a set of jewels.   Diamonds are almost *indispensible* to persons moving in good
society, whether married or single, and it is
the usual custom for a mother to present
each of her daughters with a small set of
them, as she emerges from childhood.   Yet
with all this magnificence the Portugueze
ladies do not dress well; their clothes are generally ill chosen and by no means becoming
to the figure, and they mingle all colours of
the rainbow without any scruple.   The

French modistes settled in Lisbon, charge
exorbitantly for every fresh fashion; but
they appear to me to be very inferior in talent and in taste to those of Paris or London.
The quantity of false curls and braids of hair
worn by every woman is really surprising;
all ranks and all ages adopt the custom: nor
is it without necessity, for the heat of the
climate inducing great perspiration, pre-
vents the natural hair from retaining its curl,
and it grows so thinly upon the forehead
and temples, as to have a very disagreeable
bald effect, unless assisted by art. I had
formerly heard that the length and luxuriance of the hair was a chief feature in
the beauty of Portugueze ladies; but this
appears, from all I have been able to observe,
to be a total mistake. The *length*, indeed,
is always considerable, because the hair is
suffered to grow from the earliest period
of childhood; and I have often seen female
infants of two years old, with their little
tresses tied up behind in a knot, with coloured ribbands: but the *thickness* is not genuine,
and where it appears so, it almost always
proceeds from the mere *coarseness* of the

176   CINTRA.

hair. The art of the Friseur being a refinement, of course you will not be surprised to
hear that there is not one good *professor* in
Lisbon; they do not even know how to cut
hair properly. I ought to add, however,
that I have seen several exceptions to what
I have just said, among ladies with whom I
am acquainted.

A letter from Mr. B. which I have just
received, gives an account of his feelings
upon having seen the interior of the inquisition at Lisbon.   He says : " The Inquisition
is now open to the free inspection of the
public, and I bore the most disgusting effluvia that can be imagined from the most
filthy of mobs, in order to pay minute attention to the horrors of that iniquitous place !
In one dismal dungeon lay the skulls and
bones of several victims, and more have been
discovered *between the walls* of the cells :
on one of the walls was engraved the name
of an unfortunate Englishman; but he is now
at rest from the rage of his merciless perse-
cutors, in a land where no inquisitor is permitted to enter. I have seen public executions
of different kinds, but nothing in the nature

of punishment has ever yet made so strong an impression upon my mind, as the view of this detestable prison. I felt that I was walking upon ground which formerly had been trodden only by the cruel or the unhappy! During the whole time I passed here, the image of corporal Trim's poor " brother Tom" was continually before my eyes. The people are furiously active in tearing down the walls of the place, in order to discover the remains of other victims to superstition and revenge." It is said, that no action of atrocity has been committed by the Portugueze inquisitors for the last fifty years; perhaps an inspection of the bones found in these cells might, by scientific persons, be made the means of ascertaining this very doubtful point. I have already formerly mentioned that there are several horrid reports in circulation, relative to a later period of its reign; but as I heard this from a violent Constitutionalist, perhaps the statement might have been exaggerated: at all events the Cortes are right in thus exposing the system in all its horrors, and I think it one of the most poli-

178   CINTRA.

tic measures they have lately taken. How
is it possible to feel any compassion for the
present mortifications of Ferdinand of Spain,
when we recollect, that the first act of his
renewed reign was the restoration of the
inquisition of that country? If the delu-
sions of party spirit could for a moment be
put aside, there would be but *one answer* to
this question. The anecdotes circulating
here relative to the disposition and conduct
of that wretched tyrant, really make humanity shudder, and such a mixture of meanness
falsehood, and fiendish cruelty, as they display, I never could have *imagined*.

We purpose leaving Cintra on Monday
next, for the season of rain is daily expected, and the atmosphere of Lisbon is become
much cooler. I shall quit this beautiful
place without regret ; for the separation of
our domestic establishment is in every way
so unpleasant, that the charm of mere
scenery, however great, is no compensation.
Adieu.

LETTER XXIV.

Cintra, September, 1821.

WE went the other evening, to Ramallão,
a palace and gardens belonging to the queen;
the grounds are laid out in the ancient
Dutch style, and the palace on the outside,
(for we were not allowed to enter,) appears
but a shabby and tasteless residence; many
of the houses belonging to the first nobility
have this exterior effect, and the utter
want of comfort and delicacy is evident at
the first glance, from the filthy dung heaps
which are for ever found, (undisturbed by
a broom or any other scavenger than *the
dogs*,) lying beneath the windows of the best
apartments: a number of fowls are always
kept by every family, whether rich or poor,
and as they never make any use of the
feathers, they are suffered to remain un-
collected; by which means an accumulation

N 2

180   CINTRA.

of fleas and vermin is infallibly induced, which
sometimes rises to the torment of an Egyptian plague: I shall never forget seeing the
Count de—— for the first time, in the fore-
noon of a very hot day, standing out in a
balcony of his *palace* as it is called, (a building which, however spacious, had all the air
of a sordid gloomy dilapidated prison,)
dressed in his usual morning dishabille,
hands face and teeth unwashed, hair in disorder, and with a swarthy beard which evidently had not felt a razor for two or three
days, a tooth-pick in his mouth, which (as
Malvolio seems to think) is a great and
dignified resource for idle persons of high
rank, and hanging over the fumes of one of
the largest heaps of impurity, that I had
yet seen, even in the filthiest streets of
Lisbon; such a specimen of a nobleman
and his palace, was indeed not to be passed
over without due wonder and admiration!

I have seen a singular equipage, belonging
to a gentleman of the neighbourhood who
has a large family, but who cannot afford
to keep horses or mules for their accommodation; a clumsy old coach, (as large as

a travelling caravan at an English fair, or a barge,) drawn by *bullocks*. This ponderous machine is well suited to the state of the roads in Portugal, (which are all dreadfully rough and dangerous,) and I dare say it would contain three times the number of persons, who were stowed, as the poet informs us, in the chaise of Johnny Gilpin's wife. This Noah's ark stopped at the gates of several houses here, and the door was with some difficulty wrenched open by the driver, (*drover* I ought to say,) who also enacted the part of footman. I must own, I should greatly enjoy seeing a London fine lady condemned to make her round of visits in a similar vehicle, after having been accustomed all her life to the Sybarite indulgence of her vis-a-vis, lined with eider down, and hung upon springs of the best workmanship: let it not be imagined that the antediluvian coach in question was merely a *country* contrivance, for the same sort of things are frequently seen even in the streets of the fashionable metropolis of Lisbon. As far as my own experience goes, I am inclined to believe that I was told nothing but the

182   CINTRA.

truth, when it was said that the higher
classes of females in Portugal are almost
always plain; we have lately been introduced
to a few donnas, who have the reputation
of beauty; Rubens perhaps might have
admired their persons, which were full, even
to excess, although he would have found no
tints of complexion worthy the emulation of
his pencil; as to my own opinion, I must
confess, that I thought their face and form
highly inelegant and clumsy, and that I
am utterly at a loss to conceive how it is
possible to think these ladies beautiful; one
of them came with her husband to pass a
few days in the rural retirement of Cintra,
and appeared at eleven o'clock in the fore-
noon, with diamond earings, and her fingers
covered with the most superb rings.   There
is one young lady here, who forms the
greatest exception to the generality of her
countrywomen that I have yet seen; her
delicate features, graceful manners, and
tasteful neatness and simplicity of dress,
would do honour to any country; but I
ought, in justice, to mention that she has

been educated by an English governess.
The Viscondessa de L—— has just returned
from paying her duty at Queluz; the first
time her age and infirmities have allowed of
her doing so, since the return of the royal
family: she still holds a nominal appoint-
ment at the palace, which is only conferred
upon persons of a certain rank, and yet
this " illustrious" lady does not know how
to spell her own name, or to write a note
without offending against the commonest
rules of grammar; her case is by no means
singular, as many noble compatriots can
keep her in countenance; you may judge
by this, of the state of education among the
nobility, under the ancienne regime: she
was so obliging as to show me her court
dress, which is one of a *livery* common to
all persons who are in waiting upon the
king or queen; nothing can be more ugly,
or in a worse taste; a train of red silk, of
the flimsy Portugueze manufacture, and a
petticoat of dark dull blue, of the same
material; one embroidered in gold, the other
in silver, at the edges; with which is worn

184   CINTRA.

(by all but widows,) a head-dress of red and white feathers; widows always appear in a cap, with black flowers.

The silk fabric at Lisbon is said to be improving, particularly during the last twelve months, and there is certainly great need of it; I have seen specimens of their very best silk and satin, which were both rich and thick, although without lustre (comparatively speaking) and extremely dear. French silks are strictly prohibited, but they are not the less worn and admired by the belles of fashion. The national colours are now changed to light blue and white, and the king himself has submitted to wear the cockade, composed of them. Had his majesty *originally* given half of what is now wrested from his grasp, the people would have adored him, and he might have retained all the best and most truly noble attributes of a sovereign; as it is, he gains nothing by the most abject compliances, but the contempt of both parties, Corcunda and Liberal; he is said to have been warned of the probability of the present Revolution,

CINTRA.   **185**

many years ago, by a few calm and rational
thinkers who were attached to his interests;
but he continued unfortunately deaf to all
advice, until the event actually took place,
when the favourable moment was over, and
his prospects closed—(it *may* be) for ever.
Adieu.

———

LETTER XXV.

Buenos Ayres, October 18th.

WE arrived here last Monday; the weather is highly agreeable, for the heat has
greatly subsided, and I was impatient to
return to Lisbon, as my husband's official
duties confine him so much, that I have
seen but little of him at Cintra: the periodical rains are expected immediately, and
people seem to think it unusual, that they
have not already set in.

This day is marked by peculiar solemnity:
there has been a grand funeral service performed, in the fine church of San Domingo,
and masses said for the souls of the twelve
patriots, with the intrepid General Freire at
their head, who, four years ago, perished
upon the scaffold, martyrs in the cause of
their oppressed and degraded country. It
is a pity that the *seed* sown by these devoted
men, should now be reaped by the present

government, whose character and talent are
so far inferior; I really cannot forgive the
Cortes, for their self-interested arrogant
narrow-minded policy; they have by chance
been raised to the possession of that absolute power, which in wise and virtuous
hands would have been exercised in the
cause of humanity, justice and reason; *much*
might have been effected for the welfare
and happiness of the people, and *so little*
in fact has been attempted, that my heart
sickens, and my indignation burns, whenever my thoughts turn upon the subject;
the persons now at the head of affairs (independent of their more serious defects,)
seem to think, (in common with all minds
of a limited order,) that arrogance is dignity, and they adapt their practice to their
theory, upon all occasions; had the king
more energy, his cause might certainly regain the ascendency, when it is to be hoped
that past sufferings would teach him to
fulfil with more effect, the sacred duties of
a sovereign. It is the fashion in these revolutionary times, to sneer at the term *"sacred"*
as applied to majesty; and yet, if we refer

to the eternal laws of order and truth, (which latter is but another name for justice,) we cannot avoid perceiving that a *king*, when he scrupulously fulfils the various and important duties imposed by the Almighty at the moment he placed a crown upon his brow, merits from all good men that solemn and affecting appellation. I must confess, that I am primitive enough to think, and sometimes courageous enough to assert, that it is from a forgetfulness of, and a departure from the plain straight-forward paths of religion, that monarchy has fallen of late into such disrepute; I attribute its evident decline to no secondary cause, and I am hopeless of the future amelioration or happiness of the world, while persons in power, shall continue to uphold the infamous yet recieved maxim of government, that " what is *morally wrong*, may or *can* be *politically right*. " The advice to kings and governors, which the excellent Fenelon has given in the pages of his Telemachus, ought to be engraven in letters of gold and fire, in the halls and upon the hearts of every sovereign; we *now* consider his work merely as a *juve-*

nile class book; alas! the time may come,
when the greyheaded wise ones will regret
that they have so utterly despised the
lessons taught in this school; sooner or later
we shall all be forced back by the invincible
course of events, by the stemless tide of
truth, to the same point from which we first
departed, and from which we ought never
to have diverged; but alas, what tragedies
may occur, ere the salutary return is effected! You will not accuse me of romance,
or fanaticism, in what I have just said, for
I have only urged the sentiments of that
divine lawgiver, whose words are those of
" eternal truth and life!"

The Spanish ambassador and his countess
are just gone, having concluded their mission, which was to offer congratulations to
the king and royal family, upon their return
from the Brazils; the *graceful* Spaniard,
(for such indeed the countess really is,) came
to bid us farewell, previous to their journey,
and in the fashion of her country, repeatedly
kissed me on both cheeks, embracing me in
the most engaging manner, and offering to
execute any commissions for us at Madrid;

190   LISBON.

I regret her departure, for we were just commencing an acquaintance, and found her society very promising.   Another diplomatic friend, with whom we were more intimate, is also about to leave us for his own court; he dislikes Lisbon as much we do, and laughs extremely at the enthusiasm of those English travellers, who have imposed on their fire-side friends at home, by representing it as a sort of " *Pays de Cocagne.*"   This evening, I have received a visit from a lady of one of the first houses in Portugal; the Condeça d'A. who is just returned to her Lisbon residence, after a sejour of many months at her estate in a distant province; she is the first, (with the exception of the la C——s,) who has shown us the smallest attention or civility upon our arrival in this " land of the stranger:" but why should I mention civility or hospitality towards foreigners? they seem to be virtues *unknown* to this people, generally speaking; the Condeça has invited us to her house, (I believe at the instigation of our mutual diplomatic friend, to whom I have lately alluded,) on all nights, except those on which there is an opera, as she tells me she is a constant attendant at San Carlos: her first appearance possessed considerable novelty for an English eye, as she was ornamented with many fine jewels, (among which I remarked a brilliant pin of a single stone, as large as a hazel nut,) and decorated with the order of St. John, enriched with diamonds, which she wore at her bosom; she is the only female (with the exception of one other lady of high rank,) upon whom the grand-master had conferred such a distinction; being a widow, her dress was black, as in this country the relict never re-assumes colours after the demise of the husband, unless she is either very young, or has no shame in rendering it apparent to the eyes of the world that she wishes to marry again.

It is really surprising to observe the number of jewels worn by the *inferior* classes also; the chambermaid at the hotel at Cintra wore real diamond earings when she was dressed for mass, and when I was at the fair of Campo Grande (the largest in Portugal, and much frequented by all ranks,) I saw

192   LISBON.

a common huckstress standing behind her
shopboard in a paltry booth, selling linen-
drapery, who wore the most brilliant diamond
drops in her ears, of such enormous length,
that they nearly touched her collar bones;
she was also adorned with a Brazilian chain,
(always of the purest gold,) which appeared
to be several yards long. The communica-
tion between this country and the Brazils,
(which latter seems to be a kind of El
Dorado,) in some measure accounts for
such luxury of ornament. A friend who
called upon us this morning, mentioned the
following as the present opinion of the Portugueze in general, always excepting the
Corcundas, (who would go on hoping to see
the ancient despotism restored, though it
were effected by the ruin of the congregated
inhabitants of the world,) that "the allied
Sovereigns will not attempt any measures
hostile to the new found liberties of Spain
and Portugal; that even, were they ever so
well inclined to intermeddle, the *people* of
their respective countries would rise to prevent them, and that in a very few years the
independence of the South American go-

vernments will be acknowledged by the different European powers, and I am, indeed, very much inclined to join in this idea; time only will discover the justice of these opinions. The first and most probable disaster that is expected to happen to Portugal, is the defection of her American colonies, as a strong spirit of independence has lately been manifest among them: certain it is, that they have long been able to do without the protection of Portugal, and indeed yield far greater advantage than they receive. How long, therefore, they may continue voluntarily to submit to the yoke of the mother country, appears very problematical. The Prince Regent at Rio, Don Pedro, has always been upon bad terms with the King his father, and therefore it will not be surprising, if he should, eventually, embrace the opportunity of becoming the head of a new and independent constitutional government, should the Brazilians afford him the means. At a late meeting of the Cortes, (which now assembles in the convent of the Necessidades,) the Brazilian deputies hardily confronted those of Portugal, and from the speeches which passed between them, it was *evident* that the latter were suspicious and secretly afraid of the former, who, on their parts, took little pains to conceal their feelings of scorn and defiance.

I have alluded to the fair of Campo Grande: this is held once every year in a large open space, about two leagues from Lisbon, planted with small trees in formal avenues. There are no amusements of any sort; neither shews, swings, tumblers, jugglers, strolling actors, nor wild beasts, and worse than all, no Punchinello was to be seen. The people displayed nothing of that light mirth and bounding springing hilarity which, at meetings of a similar kind in Spain, France, and some parts of Italy, are so delightful to witness: in fact, it is nothing but a vast commercial mart, where the jeweller's booths were better supplied and more numerous than any others, and the display of English goods very considerable. The fruit stalls were also well furnished, but altogether, it was the dullest assemblage of the kind that can well be imagined, and the poisonous breaths of the mob (proceeding from their garlic-eating propensity) were, to a stranger, absolutely overpowering.

You will, perhaps, wonder that I have not yet visited Mafra; but you would cease to do so, if you were aware of the fatigue of the journey in this climate, and the total absence of all accommodations when you arrive there. It takes up an entire day to see it, on account of the considerable distance from Lisbon and the horrible road through which you must necessarily pass. During the heat of summer it is doubly formidable, as there is not a single tree to shelter the traveller from the sun's intolerable blaze; and when he at length reaches Mafra through all these difficulties, there is no inn to receive him, and if he has not had the prudence to carry provisions with him, he will run great risk of starvation, as it is nearly impossible to procure any thing really fit to eat in the place. Those persons who wish to enjoy Mafra, should take care to be invited to dine and sleep at the quinta of some friend in the neighbourhood, where, however, they might chance to pay for their meal, by being themselves devoured during the

o 2

196   LISBON.

night by bugs, &c.   Truly I am of opinion,
from all I have heard of it, that Mafra
would not compensate for the trouble of the
journey thither; not that I mean to depre-
ciate its merits as a very fine building, and
were it any thing similar to Batalha indeed,
I might risk all or any inconvenience to have
the gratification of beholding it; but I am
assured that this is by no means the case,
and therefore I feel less shame in yielding to
that physical indolence which is fast advanc-
ing upon me.

LETTER XXVI.

Buenos Ayres, Oct. 25th.

I WENT the day before yesterday to return the visits of Miss K. (sister to the Swedish Chargé here) and of the Condeça d'A.—The house of the latter commands the finest view of the Tagus and the distant mountains that we have yet seen, and I readily acknowledge that the prospect is truly grand and beautiful *in its way*. The mansion, built within the last two years by the Condeça herself, is far more cheerful and fresh in its exterior, than those of the usual run of palaces in this country, but it has no pretension to architectural ornament. The men servants who came out to receive us were numerous, but not dressed with that attention to neatness and spruceness which is so universal among the domestics of noble and wealthy families in England. The interior of the house was both superb and

convenient, and reflected great credit upon
the taste of the amiable mistress. Its apartments were many in number, all handsome,
well proportioned, and furnished with much
elegance and splendour. The estates of the
A—— family are numerous, and the principal seat, near Coimbra, is, we are assured,
one of the wonders of Portugal, and
here there has been likewise introduced a
degree of comfort as well as magnificence,
which assimilates very nearly with English
taste and ideas.*   At the Lisbon residence
she possesses a fine collection of paintings
by the old Italian masters, among which we
recognized Corregio and Michael Angelo.
She has also a private theatre here, in which
her three daughters have sometimes performed operas, as they are all extremely

---

* The kitchen of this place is a great curiosity; of
immense dimensions, and most superbly appointed.
A river flows through the midst of it, from which it is
the common practice of the cooks to catch the fish,
which a few moments afterwards are prepared for the
table. The Duke of Wellington is said to have amused
himself by fishing here, during the time that he was so
hospitably and enthusiastically received by the family.

fond of music; it is beautifully fitted up, and we were rejoiced to learn that it is her intention to open it for entertainments of this nature, during the winter. We perceived at once, that the mind of this lady, superior by nature, had received a degree of culture and polish very rare among her country women, and that she had amply benefited by the opportunities she formerly enjoyed of acquiring information by foreign travel. Her sleeping apartment opens into a room furnished with books, and I saw maps &c. lying about upon her writing table—a miracle in Portugal. Nothing could be more politely winning than her reception; and the dignity of her person, the regularity of her features, and the sweet expression of her animated countenance, harmonized entirely with the grace and ease of her manner. Her daughters seem to emulate her example; they are very young, but still they are what is called here grown up, and the eldest is recently married to her uncle by the father's side; this, however strange to our apprehensions, has every appearance of being a happy and prudent match, as the young

200 LISBON.

lady is *attached* to her husband, and the gentleman still in the prime of middle age, and of an estimable character and temper. The second daughter is remarkable, from the fair bloom of her complexion, her blue eyes and light brown hair, all of which are uncommon in this "land of the sun." The Condeça herself was married very early in life to a near relation, who was at the same time far advanced in years; and it is but too usual for young girls of high rank to be disposed of by their parents, for their own inclinations are seldom consulted, at the age of twelve and thirteen, to very old men, the pope readily consenting to grant dispensations which enable such marriages to take place. A noble foreigner, of very intelligent and agreeable manners, who has passed several years in the Brazils, tells me, that in Portugueze society there, the utmost form and ceremony prevail; when you enter a room every body rises, and it is expected that you should be particularly minute in inquiring after the health of every absent connection of the mistress of the house. You must always visit in full dress, as if decorated for court, and make about a hundred bows and curtsies at coming in and going away, or else resign yourself to the mortification of being considered as wholly ignorant and ill-bred. He added, that he would not advise an English friend to look for conversation, in the true sense of the term, at any of these meetings, for the thing is unknown.

We went afterwards to purchase some trifles at a jeweller's shop in the Rua d'Ouro (Gold-street) who is reckoned the Gray or Rundel of Lisbon; we saw several handsome ornaments and magnificent stones, but nothing could bear the smallest comparison in point of workmanship, fancy, or taste, with the beautiful things to be met with in London or Paris. We had occasion to remark, (of what, indeed, we had often been assured,) " the ridiculous pomposity, inattention, and disrespect of the tradesmen in Lisbon;"— they generally conceive that they are doing you a favour in allowing you to purchase of them, and if you enter a shop and inquire if they have such and such an article, they will sometimes answer " yes," but without giving themselves the trouble of bringing it for your inspection, unless you directly request that they will do so.* An English lady purchased a pair of diamond earrings of the little Don Pomposo to whom I have just alluded; they amounted to more than ten guineas in value, nor did she attempt to object to their price, yet he received her money with almost a sneer upon his countenance, and wholly disdained to thank her as she left the shop: to this circumstance we were ourselves witnesses. The Portugueze manufacture cotton prints, muslins and calicoes, but they are far behind those of England: woollen goods are also of a very inferior quality, flannel in particular being both dear and bad; much of the latter useful article comes from our own country, but the Portugueze rarely import the best sort.

Driving through the city the other day, we encountered a very common, yet, to a stranger, a most unpleasant sight: two women in an open sege, at whose feet, rolling

---

* This peculiarity must, I should think, have been handed down to them from the Moors, as it is well known to exist among that people.

about with every motion of the carriage, lay
the uncovered corpse of a young child, wrap-
ped in a tawdry shawl of orange coloured silk,
and loaded with other trumpery finery. Infants, whose parents cannot well afford the
expense of a funeral, are taken generally,
to the see, or cathedral church of Lisbon,
and left on the steps, or upon some tomb, to
be interred at the convenience of the priest.
The nuns and other charitable persons take
pleasure in decking the little corpse with all
the finery they can collect, and these fallen
blossoms are called "angelios," (angels,)
while their death, when under the age of seven years, is considered as a signal favour
from heaven, and kept as a festival by the
parents. In one of the city churches, a few
days since, a poor woman had left the body
of her child, and not finding it buried at the
time she expected, took it home for the night
and returned it the next morning. The ra-
pacious padres of this superstitious country
will rarely do their duty without payment of
some sort; and it occasionally happens that
a dead body is seen lying on its back in the
open streets, with a little cup or pan placed

upon the breast, for the reception of voluntary subscriptions to defray the expenses of
burial.   An English acquaintance of ours,
who certainly is not too partial tô this people,
was narrating some curious anecdotes illus-
trative of their manners and customs, and
more particularly mentioned the. disgusting
scenes which `are sometimes witnessed at
these funerals.   Should the rank or circumstances of the deceased have been at all respectable, he is carried with great pomp to the
grave, attended by many persons bearing
lighted torches or wax tapers, and followed
by other mourners: when they reach the
place of interment, the grave is opened, and
the corpse taken out of the *long trunk* in
which it had been previously contained, and
thrown heedlessly into it, frequently without
even the decency of a shroud.

   The priests are generally very active in ob-
taining rich bequests from their dying peni-
tents, but now and then they are paid by the
latter in their own coin: an instance of this
is just come to our knowledge, at which I
confess I was wicked enough to laugh very
heartily.—A sick gentleman of considerable

property thinking himself at the last extremity, called in two of these reverend advisers, who persuaded him, during a violent paroxysm of pain, to vow a pair of silver candlesticks to Saint Antonio (their patron) in case he should recover. Shortly afterwards he got well, and was duly reminded of his promise. "Certainly," said he, "it is already fulfilled ;—it was the first step I took upon recovering my health: look here."—Then, leading them to a table, he pointed out a pair of silver candlesticks, about two inches in height, and not thicker than a straw, which were placed before a miniature of St. Antonio, which he himself possessed.

The Chagas church is enriched by the votive offerings of native mariners, who, during a storm, are wont to promise to their favourite saint, the donation of their best sail, if he will extricate them from the impending danger; and it is no unusual circumstance, to see an immense sail carried up the steep ascent to this church, by a ship's crew, who immediately afterwards redeem it for a sum of money. The Cortes are at present

employed in abolishing a convent, situated at
about the distance of a mile from Lisbon, in
which the captains of vessels used invariably to confine their wives during their own
absence upon a long voyage.   Whatever
may have been the iniquities of the Inquisition, some small apology may fairly be offered, on the plea of the darkness of the ages
in which they prospered most; but cruelties
of quite as deep a die are still perpe-
trated in some of the convents of modern
days.   It was only a week ago, that a monk
was discovered in a loathsome dungeon in
one of them, where he had been confined
for some venial offence ever since the year
1813; he had suffered so much from bad
food, want of cleanliness, and the depriva-
tion of free air, that his death almost immediately followed his release.

LETTER XXVII.

Buenos Ayres, Oct. 26th.

THE Portugueze are by no means less proud of their city, than the Spanish proverb tells us that people are of Seville; indeed they seem not at all behind the Chinese in their estimation of their own capital as the metropolis of the universe, the true centre of the " celestial empire." A little satirical work, lately published, (or republished, I know not which,) is said to have ruffled the plumes of this self-important people, though it is questioned whether they will improve by its useful hints; its title is " Adam alive again," who is supposed to be permitted to return to earth, for the purpose of making the tour of the world. Our worthy progenitor, like many other old gentlemen, is both surprised and indignant at every change that has been introduced since his

own time, considering the highest improve-
ments in the light of innovations : he passes
rapidly through England, France, Italy, Germany and other countries, and finds nothing
but perpetual subjects of annoyance; in the
remote parts of Germany, indeed, he is a
little comforted by perceiving some remains
of venerable and primitive ignorance, but
when he comes to Portugal he breathes
freely. "Here" he exclaims in a rapture,
"here will I take up my future abode; here
are no nonsensical refinements, no learning,
no science, no literature; agriculture is free
from modern presumptuous innovations, and
so far from being pestered with what are
called the 'fine arts,' I can scarcely perceive any appearance of what are denomina-
ted by the ridiculous philosophers of the
day, 'useful inventions;' the wise, the noble,
the magnanimous Portugueze have in no
respect altered since I left the world, and
they alone are worthy the honour of my
association."

Last night we were at the opera; the
house is a handsome spacious building, and

the king's box in the centre of the dress circle, of very ample dimensions, rising in a
dome to the upper tiers, has a truly splendid
and regal effect. The theatre is badly
lighted, shabby in its decorations, and dirty
in the extreme, but it possesses some scenes
beautifully executed; two large arm-chairs,
and a range of small ones, for the king,
queen, and royal family, occupy the front of
their box, behind which rises a gallery for
the ladies and gentlemen in waiting; up to
the present moment we are assured that the
latter personages, however dignified their
rank, were always obliged, by etiquette, to
stand, during the whole performance, however tedious, if they were admitted to the
honor of a place in the same box, instead of
remaining in the gallery just mentioned. We
were pleased by the performance, " La Festa
da Rosa," but our admiration was limited to
one or two of the performers. This opera
(light and brilliant in the style of its music) is
composed by Coccià, a young Italian, who
copies so closely from Rossini, that it is sometimes difficult to distinguish the difference between them; the whole company are from

VOL. I.   P

210   LISBON.

Milan, as well as the corps de ballet; the latter seem to posses little talent, and the mechanist must be, I should suppose, about the worst in Europe; as to the greater part of the scenery, and the dresses of the performers, economy appears to be the order of the day, or rather night. One thing it was impossible not to see—the ignorance, generally speaking, of the audience; almost all the applause was given to what really least deserved encouragement, and a few delicate strokes of genuine talent were entirely lost upon them. Favini was Prima Donna, her voice is much decayed, more from accident or indisposition, than from age, as she is still young and handsome enough for her profession; I should conceive that it had once been very fine; her taste is extremely good, and she is a lively graceful actress :— those who admire her most, insist that we ought to pardon the huskiness of her tones, in consideration of the injury they probably received in the bleak climate of Russia; for Favini was at Moscow with the French armies, composing part of the travelling baggage of Beauharnois.

LISBON.   **211**

In comparison with our English belles,
the present audience certainly did not look
to advantage; there is a superiority in the
former, not only in beauty, but in elegance of
dress and appearance altogether, which is
not to be mistaken: I say this, in no spirit
of unworthy and illiberal exultation, but
merely as it struck me as being a simple
truth.

Adieu.

LETTER XXVIII.

Buenos Ayres, Nov. 2d.

THIS month generally opens in Portugal during a rainy fortnight, which is the immediate precursor of St. Martin's summer; but this year the weather has been so unusually capricious, that we have only experienced two or three days of rain, at irregular intervals, and the summer of this saint seems to have arrived at least ten days before its time. The sun was unclouded yesterday, and very warm without being fierce; a fine breeze tempered its rays, and we availed ourselves of the opportunity to take an excursion by water, to return the visit of an English lady who resides at Pedroiços, a small town upon the Tagus, at a few miles distance from Lisbon, close to the picturesque

Drawn by M. Baillie.

FISHERMAN'S FAMILY OF PEDROICOS.

Published June 1834, by John Murray, London.

castle of Belem. The view of Lisbon, when seen from the river, is superbly beautiful; the white and lofty houses, free from smoke, appear as if they ought to be the favourite abodes of elegance and purity; but the moment you land, the pleasing illusion vanishes at once. When we quitted the boat at Pedroiços, we found ourselves upon the sands, close under the old Gothic castle which I have just mentioned, which is now made use of as a state prison: the Conde dos Arcos is at present confined there, having rendered himself obnoxious to the new government, upon his return from the Brazils, by the exhibition of Corcunda principles. We soon discovered the residence of Mrs. C——, which boasts of pure air, and is perfectly free from the effluvia of Lisbon or Buenos Ayres; she affirms it to be much cooler also than either, although there is nothing like shade to be seen. We observed that the fences by the road side were chiefly hedges of the aloe, which rises to an enormous height, and here and there a palm-tree reared its slender form among them, giving proof positive of the fierce degree of heat

common to this climate. The fishermen's
families chiefly reside in this neighbourhood,
and we met several of them in their peculiar
costume, carrying large baskets, or antique-
shaped pitchers of red earth, upon their
heads; the latter are made of porous clay,
and are in universal use as water-coolers;
they are, I am told, so admired by the
Italians for their classic forms, (certainly a
remnant of Roman taste,) that large quantities are frequently exported to Italy. Some
of these women were busily employed in
roasting chestnuts in the open air, and the
same trade is going on at this season in
every street of Lisbon; nothing can be more
delicious than this fruit so prepared: the
manner in which they are sent to table in
the houses of our English epicures is far
inferior; I know not the process there
employed, but the Portugueze method is
to roast them in an earthen pot, beneath
which is a pan of burning charcoal; the
women perpetually fan the reluctant embers
into a gentle blaze, sprinkling the chestnuts,
in their skins, from time to time, with the
same kind of coarse salt used in curing

their sardinhas, and which is said to give
them a peculiar flavour. The sardinha is
a small fish resembling our sprat, which at
certain seasons forms the principal food of
the lower classes in Portugal. Passing by a
shop in this marine village, we saw (for the
first time) two men dancing the national
dance, which greatly resembles the *cachucha*
of Spain, to the sound of the viola or Portugueze guitar, strung with their double
wires: they snapped their fingers in cadence
to the tune, but used no castagnets, and I
saw two boatmen engaged in the same way,
upon the deck of a small vessel at anchor;
but they were dancing (or rather stamping
and gesticulating) to their own singing;
these dances were extremely monotonous, and
destitute of all graceful animation, forming
a great contrast, I am told, to those of
Spain.

Upon our return from Pedroiços, we
dressed and went in the evening to the Condeça d'A's.; the young ladies gave us several
pretty modinhas upon the guitar, and accompanied each other in Italian duets upon
the piano-forte: they speak French, Eng-

216   LISBON.

lish, and Italian, fluently, and are particularly well-bred and obliging in their manners, although a little inclined to be shy towards us as strangers.   The hair of the
youngest is really as worthy of celebration as
the tresses of *Berenice;* of a deep rich black,
confined in graceful braids, which, if they
were released from the comb, would nearly
reach the ground.   I have taken her master to teach me to accompany my voice upon
the guitar, but have chosen the Spanish
rather than the Portugueze guitar, the former being much softer, and better adapted
to the melancholy tenderness which breathes
through most of the modinhas of this country.   The Spanish songs, I think, would
sound better upon the Portugueze instru-
ment, as they are so much more spirited and
lively in their character, and the accompaniments are generally louder, and consist, in
most instances, of certain tricks and beats,
which are omitted in the Portugueze method of playing.   Buenos Ayres becomes
more and more intolerable to me, and, I fear,
I shall never be reconciled to a permanent
residence here; but I endeavour to look on

the bright side of every object, both from duty and policy; there are some things, nevertheless, to which there is but one side, and that a very black one indeed; for example, the filthy state of most places in this neighbourhood; imagine what it is to sit, as I do, night after night in the Hotel, smelling eau de Cologne, or burning dried lavender, to avoid being suffocated by the poisonous odours which, rising from the street beneath, reach to the height of our windows, and penetrate even through the panes of glass ; it has such an overpowering effect upon my nerves, that I have sometimes found it impossible to refrain from absolute tears of disgust; when we walk out also, either to attend the English chapel, or to take a boat at the water-side, we are obliged to pass through such revolting paths, that my promenade becomes a sensible penance, an absolute state of physical suffering. What I am now saying, is not at all an exaggeration, but no person who has not lived here, can form any idea of these annoyances, although they are by no means so great or so nume-

218   LISBON.

rous, as they were some few years since. An
attempt at cleanliness was first introduced by
the French, who ordered all the dogs to be
shot, and obliged the natives to exert human
labour, in cleansing the streets from the worst
species of impurity; but after the departure
of these salutary task-masters, the Portugueze once more returned to their dogs and
their dirt: the example of the English has
since effected some amelioration in their
habits and customs; so much so indeed, that
even in the city, there are two or three
streets which are preserved by the police
in a state of comparative purity, and within
these last few months, during the dry weather, I have even seen two or three street-
sweepers; but I observe that they invariably sweep against the wind. It is
very common to see dead animals left in
the open footpaths, to the annoyance of
every passenger; but the air is so dry and
clear, and the attacks of the dogs and flies
so incessant, that in a few days the carcases
lose their offensive quality, and present nothing but bare skeletons to the view. I am

sure you must be tired of this disgusting detail; I will release you therefore, and endeavour to forget " the life which late I led," in that lovely land of my affections, in which this letter will find you.

END OF VOL. I.

EDITORIAL NOTES

p. 5, l. 3: *THE EARL OF CHICHESTER*: Thomas Pelham, second Earl of Chichester (1756–1826), a Whig politician and ex-Home Secretary under Henry Addington (1801–3) and the Joint Postmaster-General (1807–23) while the Baillies were in Portugal.

p. 8, ll. 1–2: *the Peninsular war*: This was a military conflict (1808–14) between France and the allied powers of Spain, Portugal and Britain for the control of the Iberian Peninsula and the rejection of the Napoleonic forces, which tried to invade both Peninsular countries. The British and the Portuguese armies secured Portugal, using it as a safe position from which to launch campaigns against the French army in Spain. The burden of war destroyed the social and economic fabric of Portugal and Spain and ushered in an era of social turbulence, political instability and economic stagnation. The cumulative crises, revolution and restoration led to the independence of most of Spain's American colonies and the independence of Brazil from Portugal. For more information, see D. Gates, *The Spanish Ulcer* (London: Pimlico, 2002); I. Robertson, *Wellington at War in the Peninsula* (Barnsley: Pen & Sword, 2000) and R. Southey, *History of the Peninsular War* (London: John Murray, 1828). For travel books set against the backdrop of the Peninsular War, see J. Alberich, *Bibliografía anglo-hispánica, 1800–1850: Ensayo bibliográfico de libros y folletos relativos a España e Hispanoamérica impresos en Inglaterra en la primera mitad del siglo XIX* (Oxford: Dophin Books, 1978) and *A Guerra Peninsular en Portugal – Relatos Britânicos* (coord. Maria Leonor Machado de Sousa; Casal de Cambra: Caleidoscópio, 2007).

p. 8, ll. 14–18: *The absence of the sovereign ... the principal nobility*: The Portuguese royal family and their court moved to Brazil in 1808 and stayed there throughout the Peninsular War, only returning in 1821.

p. 9, ll. 10–11: *'Recollections of the Peninsula'*: Mrs Baillie is referring to M. Sherer's *Recollections of the Peninsula. By the Author of Sketches in India; Campaign of the Left Wing of the Allied Army, in the Western Pyrenees and South of France, in the Years 1813–14; under Field-Marshal the Marquess of Wellington. Illustrated by a detailed Plan of the Operations, and numerous Plates of Mountain and River Scenery, drawn and etched by Captain Batty, of the First or Grenadier Guards, F.R.S., &c. &c.* (London: Longman, Hurst, Reed, Orme and Brown, 1824). It was a very popular adventure book in its day, describing the arduous life of a soldier serving with the Border Regiment in Portugal and Spain.

p. 9, l. 17: coleur de rose: 'a bed of roses' (literally 'of rose colour') (French).

p. 10, l. 9: *'When all things please, for life itself is new'*: This quote comes from *A Clergyman's Widow and her Young Family*, published anonymously (by Mrs Barbara Hofland) in 1812. It became a popular book throughout the nineteenth century, proof of this is the fact that it was republished (now with the author's name) in 1825, 1841, 1866 and 1870. Mrs Baillie was familiar with the anonymous first edition of the book.

p. 10, ll. 16–17: *Mr Matthews, in his 'Diary of an Invalid'*: Mrs Baillie is alluding to *The Diary of an Invalid; Being the Journal of a Tour in Pursuit of Health in Portugal, Italy, Switzerland, and France in the Years 1817, 1818, and 1819*, by H. Matthews (London: John Murray, 1820, 2nd edn in 1822).

p. 13, ll. 3–4: *the King of Portugal*: The King of Portugal who Mrs Baillie is describing was D. João VI (1767–1826). He became King of Portugal in 1816, while he was still residing in Brazil. He returned to Portugal as a king in 1821.

p. 14, ll. 4–8: *A very amiable authoress ... the defection of the Brazils from the mother country*: Mrs Baillie is referring to Mrs Maria Graham (later Lady Maria Callcott), who authored *Journal of a Voyage to Brazil, and Residence There during Part of the Years 1821, 22, and 23; Including an Account of the Revolution which Brought About the Independence of the Brazilian Empire* (London: Longman, Hurst, Rees, Orme, Brown, and Green, and John Murray, 1824).

p. 14, ll. 15–16: *any unnatural warfare between father and son may be prevented*: The author is referring to D. João VI (the father) and his son D. Pedro, Regent of Brazil since 1821.

p. 18, ll. 16–17: *'helps' in America*: euphemistic term employed in America for 'helpers in the house', that is, servants, maids, and so forth.

p. 21, l. 13: *China roses*: *rosa chinensis*, an ornamental plant originating in China, with five pink to red petals.

p. 23, l. 6: *Gil Blas*: The author is alluding to the main picaresque character of A.-R. Lesage's novel *L'Histoire de Gil Blas de Santillane* (1715–35).

p. 23, l. 18: *Joseph I*: D. José I (1714–77), known in Portuguese history as 'o Reformador', was King of Portugal from 1750 to 1777. His fame as 'reformer' comes from charging the Marquês de Pombal with the reconstruction of the centre of Lisbon after its destruction in the earthquake of 1755. José I's statue was erected in 1775.

p. 23, ll. 20–1: *Machado de Castro*: Joaquim Machado de Castro (1731–1822) was the sculptor of the equestrian statue of D. José I. He also wrote a detailed description of his work in *Descripção analytica da execução da estatua equestre* (Lisbon, 1810).

p. 24, l. 1: *the Inquisition*: The Inquisition in Portugal was abolished in 1821.

p. 24, ll. 2–3: *(like the ancient lion in the fable), shorn of its terrible teeth and claws*: The author is alluding to Aesop's fable of the lion in love. Having fallen in love with a girl, her parents obliged the lion to cut his claws and teeth to avoid damaging the bride. When he did so, the bride's parents could now reject him as he was devoid of his natural weapons.

p. 24, ll. 10–14: *The people of Lisbon ... 'babbled of them'*: In Shakespeare's *Henry V* (V.ii) the character of Mother Quickly laughs at Falstaff's nose by calling it a table covered with green skin, but an old editor of Shakespeare's play could have made a mistake and transcribed 'green-fields' instead of 'green skin'. Lewis Theobald (1688–1744) made an addition to correct this blunder and Pope seemed to admit this emendation, but Dr Johnson did not. Hence the English scholar's popular reputation for hating vegetables. For more information, see E. G. Fogel's '"A Table of Green Fields": A Defence of the Folio Reading', *Shakespeare Quarterly*, 9:4 (Autumn 1958), pp. 485–92.

p. 24, ll. 15–16: *the great earthquake*: This refers to the Lisbon earthquake of 1755 which destroyed most of the city of Lisbon and was followed by a tsunami.

p. 24, ll. 17–21: *Gold Street and Silver Street ... tradesmen of that description*: Mrs Baillie uses the English translations of the original Portuguese names of these streets: Rua d'Ouro, Rua da Prata, and so forth.

p. 25, l. 12: *'Contrabandistas'*: Spanish and Portuguese for 'smugglers'.

p. 26, l. 21: *hock*: white wine from the Rhine area.

p. 26, ll. 24–5: *vinho do têrmo*: local wine of the most recent vintage.

p. 27, l. 21: *Camoens*: Luis de Camões (1524–80) is considered to be Portugal's national poet. He was the author of the epic poem *Os Lusíadas* (1572).

p. 28, l. 12: *our St. Giles*: The Greek-born St Giles (known in Latin records as Aegidius) died in France in the eighth century. His festival day in the Church of England is 1 September. He is the patron saint of beggars, cripples, the physically and mentally disabled, lepers and paupers.

p. 31, l. 5: *The Concundas, or ultras*: 'Corcundas' ('hunch–backed' in Portuguese) was the term employed by the Brazilian independentists to refer to the Portuguese who were against the independence of Brazil.

p. 33, l. 4: *Pomona*: Roman goddess of fruit, gardens and orchards.

p. 34, l. 16: *Don João*: In Portuguese the king is referred to as 'Dom João'. 'Don' is Spanish.

p. 35, ll. 6–7: *The royal family consists of two sons and four daughters*: When Mrs Baillie was in Portugal, King D. João VI had five living daughters (D. Maria Teresa, D. Maria Francisca de Assis, D. Isabel Maria, D. Maria da Assunçao and D. Ana de Jesus Maria) and two sons (one in Brazil, D. Pedro, and the other one in Portugal, D. Miguel). D. João had one more son and one more daughter (D. Francisco António, who died in 1801 at the age of six, and D. Maria Isabel, who died in 1818 at the age of twenty-one).

p. 35, ll. 17–18: *the patriarch (the Pope of Portugal)*: The patriarch of Lisbon at the time was Cardinal Carlos da Cunha e Menezes, who held the post from 1819 to 1825.

p. 36, ll. 26–6: *Mr. de Visme*: Gerard de Vismes (1726–98) was a philanthropist and British ambassador in Lisbon.

p. 38, ll. 20–2: *I agree with Mr. Matthews ... in Lisbon*: She is referring to the aforementioned *Diary of an Invalid*, p. 36. See note to p. 10, ll. 16–17, above.

p. 47, ll. 8–9: *'a second Daniel!'*: Mrs Baillie uses an expression employed by Shylock in Shakespeare's *The Merchant of Venice* to compliment Portia (disguised as a judge) on her sage judgment. Later Cassanio uses it to mock the Jew after Portia's turn of judgment to save Antonio's life. Mrs Baillie's intention is to complement her English doctor for his verdict that she and her son should be soon removed from Lisbon due to its unhealthy weather and insalubrious conditions. She is so thankful for this recommendation that she even calls him 'Saint W****' (l. 13), though his name is not specified.

p. 47, l. 17: *Doctor Sangrado*: An incompetent Spanish doctor in Lasage's *L'Histoire de Gil Blas de Santillane* for whom the protagonist, Gil Blas, works for some time.

p. 49, ll. 7–8: *the English frigate, the Liffley, Captain Duncan*: According to J. Marshall's *Royal Naval Biography: or, Memoirs of the Services of All the Flag Officers [etc.]* (London: Longman, Hurst, Rees, Orme, Brown, and Green, 1825), vol. 2, pp. 1000–1, Captain Henry Duncan (1786–1835) was briefly detached to Lisbon, where he helped to subdue a fire in a public building and also had a private audience with the king of Portugal.

p. 50, l. 12: *palace of the Ajuda*: As the Paço Real had been damaged in the earthquake of 1755, the Palacio da Ajuda was slowly built as a temporary residence for the Portuguese royal family.

p. 50, ll. 24–5: *the landing of the King ... New Government*: After Queen D. Maria I's death in 1816, Regent D. João was recognized as King of Portugal but he continued to reside in Brazil. The subsequent spread of dissatisfaction resulted in the peaceful revolution of 1820, and the proclamation of a constitutional government, to which he swore fidelity on his return to Portugal in 1822. King D. João VI landed in Lisbon on 4 July. Mrs Baillie's husband was a witness to this historical event.

p. 53, l. 7: *Rembrandt*: Rembrandt Harmenszoon van Rijn (1606–69) is the best representative painter in the history of Dutch art.

p. 54, ll. 1–2: *'pomp of groves or garniture of fields'*: a verse (book 1, canto 9, l. 4) from *The Minstrel; or, the Progress of Genius*, published in 1771–2 in two volumes, by the Scottish poet and philosopher James Beattie (1735–1803).

p. 54, l. 22: *burthen*: burden.

p. 57, l. 11: *Diogenes*: Greek philosopher known for his lack of personal hygiene.

p. 57, ll. 22–3: 'terré', 'pavé': French terms employed to indicate the parts of a constructed road.

p. 58, l. 7: *Praxitiles*: Praxiteles of Athens was a prominent sculptor of the fourth century BC. One of the most recognizable characteristics of his sculptures is the practice of the so-called 'Praxitelean curve', an elegant pose or *contrapposto* of the human figure.

p. 58, ll. 18–19: *'a rascally don peasant, stuffed with garlic'*: In Peter Motteux's very popular (though utterly faulty) English translation of *Don Quixote*, originally published in 1712, the exact quote should be 'How now, opprobrious rascal! Thou peasant stuffed with garlic'. The latest edition of *Don Quixote* in Mrs Baillie's lifetime was *The History of the Ingenious Gentleman, Don Quixote of La Mancha*; translated from the Spanish by Motteaux (Edinburgh: Hurst, Robinson, and Co.; and Archibald Constable and Co., 1822).

p. 58, ll. 20–1: *Sancho Panza*: If Don Quixote was a knight-errant, his squire (though a peasant) was Sancho Panza.

p. 60, l. 11: *the kraal of a Hottentot*: huts and surrounding enclosures of the natives of South and Central Africa.

p. 61, l. 13: *Ramalão*: Mrs Baillie refers to the Palácio de Ramalhão, a neoclassical palace in Sintra where Queen D. Carlota Joaquina, D. João VI's wife, frequently stayed after 1802, and where she was exiled after refusing to swear to the constitution of 1822.

p. 63, l. 15: *dimity*: thick cotton cloth.

P. 70, ll. 8–9: *palace of Queluz*: The Queluz Palace is an eighteenth-century Rococo palace located at Queluz, near Sintra, conceived as a summer retreat for King D. Pedro de Bragança and Queen D. Maria I. It was a discreet hiding place for Queen Maria who gradually went mad after D. Pedro's death in 1786. Following the destruction by fire of the Ajuda Palace in 1794, Queluz Palace became the official residence of the Portuguese Prince Regent, D. João and his family, until they fled to Brazil in 1807 following the French invasion of Portugal.

p. 72, l. 13: padre: 'priest': 'father' (Portuguese and Spanish).

p. 74, ll. 18–19: black *as the plumes of the gigantic helmet of Otranto*: Mrs Baillie is alluding to Horace Walpole's *The Castle of Otranto* (1764), generally considered to be the first Gothic novel, a very popular genre, widely read by women in the late eighteenth and early nineteenth centuries. The book begins on the wedding day of Conrad and Princess Isabella. Shortly before the wedding, Conrad is crushed to death by a gigantic helmet that falls on him from above.

p. 80, ll. 1–7: *The Marialva is a fine looking building ... as Childe Harold continues to be read*: *Childe Harold's Pilgrimage* (1812–18) is a travel poem written by Lord Gordon Byron. In stanza 25, ll. 1–4, Byron refers to the Convention being signed at the Palace of Marialva:

> Convention is the dwarfish demon styled
> That foil'd the knights in Marialva's dome:
> Of brains (if brains they had) he them beguiled,
> And turn'd a nation's shallow joy to gloom.

p. 80, l. 16: *formal quaint style of our William the Third*: William III of England (1650–1702) was a Protestant King of England and the House of Orange in Holland. He reigned over England in conjunction with his wife Queen Mary I, until she died in 1694. He converted to Anglicanism.

p. 80, l. 19: jet d'eau: 'jug' (French).

p. 80, l. 21: *Hampton Court*: Hampton Court Park or the Home Park is adjacent to Hampton Court Palace and Gardens in south-west London. It is a walled deer park of roughly 700 acres.

p. 80, ll. 22–5: *and brought those lines of Pope to my remembrance ... the platform just reflects the other*: These two lines (117 and 118) belong to Pope's 'Epistle IV' in his *Moral Essays*. See *The Poetical Works of Alexander Pope*. In Three Volumes. [Etc.] (Philadelphia, PA: Samuel A. Bascom, 1819), vol. 2, p. 182.

p. 81, l. 10: sérras: 'mountain range' (Portuguese).

p. 81, l. 14: '*Sierra della Ronda*': 'Serranía de Ronda', a mountain range in the province of Málaga (Spain).

p. 81, l. 15: *Sable Mountains*: This is the translation given in English for 'Sierra Morena', a mountain range that separates Castile in the centre of Spain from Andalusia in the south.

p. 81, l. 19: *Dapple*: Name given to Sancho Panza's donkey in the English translations of *Don Quixote*. The original Spanish name for his donkey was Rucio.

p. 81, l. 21: '*knight of the woeful countenance*': This is the English translation of 'El caballero de la triste figura', a description given to Don Quixote by the Bachelor Sanson Carrasco.

p. 82, l. 2: *Cardenio*: Character from Cervantes's *Don Quixote* who was self-exiled in the Sable Mountains (Sierra Morena) due to disappointments in love.

p. 82, l. 12: *Don João de Castro*: D. João de Castro was a Portuguese naval officer and eventually the fourth Viceroy of the Portuguese India (Estado Português da India), mentioned by Camões in the laudatory terms of 'Castro Forte' ('Strong Castro'). For more information on his life and deeds, see J. Freire de Andrade's *Vida de D. João de Castro* (Lisboa, 1651; translated into English by Sir Peter Wyche in 1664) and E. Sanceau's *D. João de Castro* (Porto: Livraria Civilização-Editora, 1946).

p. 86, l. 20: caressante: 'affectionate' (French).

p. 92, ll. 25–6: '*Through mud, through mire, / Over bush and over briar*': This is a personal variation of Fairy's words in Shakespeare's *A Midsummer Night's Dream* (II.i):
> Over hill, over dale,
> Through bush, through brier,
> Over park, over pale,
> Through flood, through fire,
> I do wander everywhere,
> Swifter than the moon's sphere

p. 93, l. 3: '*goblin page*': The author describes her naughty 'page' as a goblin, continuing her description of the anecdote with *A Midsummer Night's Dream's* terminology.

p. 97, l. 4: *quinta of 'Monserrat'*: quinta de Monserrate.

p. 97, ll. 20–2: *it was originally built by a rich Englishman, in the style of our own villas*: Mrs Baillie affirms that the quinta de Monserrate was built by Mr Beckford, i.e. William Beckford (1760–1844), the author of the famous Gothic novel *Vathek* (1786). Mr Beckford rented the place from another Englishman, Gerard de Vismes, who had a neo-Gothic mansion built in the quinta in 1790. In 1793 Beckford settled in Portugal for some time and used his inherited fortune to reform the palace, tidy the Romantic-looking gardens and repair a cromlech and a waterfall. It is well known that Beckford dissipated his fortune on eccentric, extravagant enterprises such as building ventures and collecting.

p. 109, ll. 8–9: Cawdies *of Edinburgh*: In *The Expedition of Humphry Clinker* (London, 1771) Tobias Smollet describes them in the following terms: 'There is at Edinburgh a society or corporation of errand-boys, called cawdies, who ply in the streets at night with paper lanthorns, and are very serviceable in carrying messages – These fellows, though shabby in their appearance, and rudely familiar in their address, are wonderfully acute, and so noted for fidelity, that there is no instance of cawdy's having betrayed his trust – Such is their intelligence, that they know, not only every individual of the place, but also every stranger, by the time he has been four and twenty hours in Edinburgh; and no transaction, even the most private, can escape their notice' (vol. 2, p. 68).

p. 109, l. 9: *Lazzaroni of Naples*: This term refers to the various kinds of lower-class street people under a 'chief' in Naples, often depicted as 'beggars', which some actually were, while others subsisted partly through their services as messengers, porters and so forth. Much and extensive information on the Lazzaroni is given in *Italy and its Inhabitants; an Account of a Tour in that Country in 1816 and 1817:* [etc], by J. Aug. Galiffe of Geneva, 2 vols (London: John Murray, 1820).

p. 109, ll. 12–13: *the province of Gallicia in Spain*: Galicia is a region in the north-west of Spain, north of Portugal, where apart from Spanish, Galician is spoken. Galician is a similar language to Portuguese. During the Middle Ages Galician-Portuguese was the same language. The Gallegos often alluded to in Mrs Baillie's work are the natives of this Spanish region.

p. 112, l. 17: *the recent Revolution*: Mrs Baillie is referring to the peaceful revolution of 1820, the so-called Porto Revolution, where the constitution was imposed on the Portuguese king D. João VI.

p. 116, ll. 6–12: *I am inclined ... mentioned by Mr. Wilks*: Mrs Baillie is referring to *History of the Persecutions Endured by the Protestants of the South of France: and more especially of the Department of the Gard, during the Years 1814, 1815, 1816, &c.: Including a Defence of their Conduct, from the Revolution to the Present Day*, by M. Wilks (London: Longman, Hurst, Rees, Orme & Brown, 1821).

p. 119, l. 16: *Tagus*: This river begins in Spain, traverses Castile, passes through Lisbon and ends in the Atlantic: it is called 'Tejo' in Portuguese, 'Tajo' in Spanish. It is the longest river in the Iberian Peninsula.

p. 121, ll. 4–8: *'Alas! she was discovered ... miserable death by inanition!'*: *Marmion* is a very successful epic poem by Walter Scott (1808). The poem tells how Lord Marmion, a favourite of Henry VIII, lusts for Clara de Clare, a rich woman. He and his mistress, Constance De Beverley, forge a letter implicating Clara's fiancé, Sir Ralph De Wilton, in treason. Constance, a dishonest nun, hopes that her aid will restore her to favour with Marmion. Constance's death in the poem is anticipated by Mrs Baillie.

p. 124, l. 8: *It is accounted rather hazardous to visit this colony*: Mrs Baillie does not indicate the name of this peculiar village on the shores of the Tagus, near Lisbon, whose inhabitants seem to be rather violent.

p. 125, l. 13: *an Atalanta*: A character in Greek mythology: a strong yet feminine woman who faces obstacles and backlash for refusing to follow gender norms, a virago.

p. 126, l. 14: *Talavera in Spain*: Talavera de la Reina, in the province of Toledo, Spain, famous for its high-quality colourful pottery.

p. 128, ll. 5–6: the village poet: The name of this local poet in Sintra in the first quarter of the nineteenth century has not been identified.

p. 128, l. 9: *Helicon*: According to Greek mythology, the name of a mountain with fountain waters that gave drinkers the ability to sing.

p. 128, l. 10: *cacoëthes scribendi*: 'insatiable urge to write' (Latin). Its origin dates back to Juvenal's *Satires*: 'tenet insanabile multos scribendi cacoethes' ('incurable urge to write affects many').

p. 128, l. 18: *melancholy Jaques*: Jaques is a character from Shakespeare's *As You Like It*. He is depicted as a moody cynic who constantly draws from life his ever-unsatisfactory poetic contemplations of the nature of the world around him.

p. 133, l. 10: *Florence or Lucca oils*: The olive oil produced from these cities was thought to be the best in Italy. It was amply celebrated by the numerous British Grand Tour travellers in Italy as light and refined.

p. 134, l. 9: *Embonpoint*: 'stout' (French).

p. 134, l. 25: *the celebrated Cork convent*: Mrs Baillie is referring to the Convento de Santa Cruz da Serra da Sintra (Convent of the Santa Cruce de Cintra, or the Convent of the Holy Cross of the Cintra Rock), famous for its subterraneous chambers and chapels and better known as the Cork Convent. Lord Byron alluded to it thus in his *Childe Harold Pilgrimage* (stanza 20): 'Below, at some distance, is the Cork Convent, where St. Honorius dug his den, over which is his epitaph.'

p. 140, ll. 1–2: *One of the late kings of Portugal was united to his* aunt: King D. Pedro III (1717–86) became King of Portugal, Brazil and the Algarves after marrying his niece D. Queen Maria I (1734–1816) in 1777.

p. 141, ll. 8–9: *venerable* Principal *of Portugal, 'Freire'*: This high-ranking ecclesiastical priest in Sintra has not been identified.

p. 144, l. 21: *late unfortunate General Freire*: Gomez Freire de Andrade (1757–1817), having supported Napoleon in the Peninsular War, was mistrusted by the Portuguese on his return to Portugal. He was accused of high treason and condemned to be shot in 1817, a few years before Mrs Baillie arrived in the area.

p. 147, l. 18: *the jolly* Father Paul: This is the main character of a popular may-day song titled 'Father Paul', whose chorus ran thus:

Here's a hearth for Father Paul,

A hearth to Father Paul,

For flowing bowls inspire the souls

Of jolly friars all.

p. 148, l. 13: *Delf ware*: Delftware is a blue and white pottery made in Delft (Holland) from the sixteenth century onwards.

p. 149, l. 4: *Vesta*: Roman goddess of home.

p. 153, ll. 11–12: *(Our Lady of the Rock)*: Mrs Baillie interprets the name of the church correctly (as she shows by including the Portuguese translation of the place). Byron had not interpreted it so well in his *Childe Harold's Pilgrimage*, stanza 10, where he translates the Portuguese 'penha' as 'punishment', and translates *Nossa Senhora da Penha* as 'Our Lady of Punishment'. For more information, see P. H. Churchman's article 'Lord Byron's Experiences in the Spanish Peninsula in 1809', *Bulletin Hispanique*, 11:1 (1909), pp. 55–95.

p. 154, l. 10: *Donnas*: 'ladies' (Italian) and 'ladies' (Portuguese, although spelt with a single 'n': 'donas'). This is a title prefixed to the first name of an Italian or Portuguese lady.

p. 154, l. 19: *soi-disant*: 'supposedly' (French). 'Soi-disant' means literally 'saying oneself'. It entered English in the seventeenth and eighteenth centuries, like hundreds of other French words and expressions, in spite of the political and military antipathies between both countries. Mrs Baillie did not learn much Portuguese during her stay in Portugal (hence her solitude and boredom) and addressed many people in French, a language that she seemed to be fluent in.

p. 155, l. 25: *La Fille de L'Air*: This is a drama written by Count Carlo Gozzi (1720–1806), one of the main Italian playwrights of the eighteenth century who tried to revitalize the *commedia dell'arte*, masques and extravagant dramatized fairy tales. He was also very influenced by Spanish Golden Age drama. For 'La fille de l'air', written in three acts and verse (performed for the first time in 1786 and published in 1791) he was inspired by Calderón de la Barca's *La hija del aire* (1653). For information on Gozzi's life and works, see G. Luciani's *Carlo Gozzi: 1720–1806, l'homme et l'œuvre* (Paris: Atelier, 1977).

p. 155, ll. 25–6: *Madame de Stael in her Corinne*: Madame de Staël (1766–1817) was a French novelist and essay writer. She was the author of *Corinne, ou l'Italie* (1807).

p. 157, ll. 12–14: *like Boniface with his ale ... and sleep upon their cards*: Mrs Baillie makes a personal adaptation of the famous saying 'fun is to me what ale was to Boniface; I sleep upon fun – I drink for fun – I talk for fun – I live upon fun' to refer to the life of leisure of most Portuguese families.

p. 157, ll. 13–14: *a country which has produced but one great author*: This one great Portuguese author is Camões.

p. 158, l. 3: *Voltaire, Diderot, &c. &c*: François Marie Aouet (1694–1778), better known as 'Voltaire', and Denis Diderot (1713–84) were two of the leading French philosophers of the Enlightenment.

p. 158, l. 25: *immortal Fenelon*: François Fenelon (1651–1715), a French Catholic theologian and poet, prophesized the outburst of a popular revolution as a punishment for the excesses of the monarchy in a famous visionary letter to King Louis XIV in 1694.

p. 159, ll. 2–3: *Spanish ambassador extraordinary, and his countess*: These attractive and appealing historical characters have not been identified.

p. 159, l. 15: appendage: literally 'appendix' (French), here meaning 'a lover', an 'accompaniment' of the opposite sex.

p. 159, l. 17: '*the* cicesbeo': During the eighteenth and nineteenth centuries the Spanish term 'chichisbeo' (from the Italian 'cicisbeo') was used to refer to the assiduous attention of a gentleman to a married woman.

p. 162, l. 18: *the Hidalgos*: the petty aristocracy (Spanish).

p. 167, l. 7: salam: term employed here in the sense of 'greeting' or 'bowing' (Arabic).

p. 168, l. 21: *Richmond*: Richmond is a wealthy area in London located on a meander of the Thames with a large number of parks, the most famous of which is Richmond Park, a fashionable place for socializing and recreation during the nineteenth century.

p. 172, ll. 22–3: *Polanders*: term for 'Pole' or 'Polish' (archaic English).

p. 174, ll. 6–7: '*Memoirs of the Margravine of Bareith', by Thibault*: Mrs Baillie is referring to *Memoirs de ma vie*, by Frederica Sophia Wilhalmine Margravine of Brandenburg-Bayreuth, Princess of Prussia. She was a Prussian princess and composer (1709–58). Her memoirs were written between 1709 and 1758 and were published in German and in French in 1810. It is recommended reading for those interested in the European court history of the age. Baron Thibault, the late Lieutenant General in the French Army, had nothing to do with the writing of the 'margravine memoirs'.

p. 178, ll. 12–13: *the Cumberland and Westmorland lakes*: Bucolic area in the north-west of England.

p. 182, l. 17: *Edinburgh and Quarterly Reviews*: The *Edinburgh Review* was founded in 1802 and was one of the most influential British magazines in the nineteenth century. The *Quarterly Review* was a literary and political periodical founded in 1809 by John Murray.

p. 182, l. 18: tyros: Mrs Baillie is referring to the Portuguese magazines as having much to learn from their British models.

p. 182, l. 19: *the New Monthly Magazine*: a British monthly magazine published by Henry Colburn in 1814.

p. 184, ll. 4–6: '*Assume the God … shake the spheres*': A quote from John Dryden's ode *Alexander's Feast; or, the Power of Music* (1697):

> With ravish'd ears
> The monarch hears,
> Assumes the god;
> Affects to nod,
> And seems to shake the spheres.

p. 185, l. 19: *nuovo cruzado*: The cruzado novo or *cruzado de prata* was worth 480 réis. Its original silver quantity and weight (17 g of high-quality silver) kept going down with time, since it was first coined during D. Pedro II's reign (1683–1706). Mr Baillie's generosity is here depicted by his wife, as a 'nuovo cruzado' was a large tip for a child.

p. 189, l. 1: *Marquis de Pombal*: D. Sebastião José de Carvalho e Melo (1699–1782) was Prime Minister during D. José I's reign. He is best remembered for his attempts at modernizing Portuguese society and for his reconstruction of Lisbon's city centre after the 1755 earthquake.

p. 189, l. 22: *Fidalga*: 'gentlewoman' (Portuguese), a female member of the Portuguese petty aristocracy.

p. 190, ll. 2–6: *Lord Ogleby …'Vulgar fellow! hot rolls and butter in July!'*: A variation of a statement made by the character of Lord Ogleby in reference to the character of Sterl, who is looking forward to having hot rolls and butter in July in David Garrick and George Colman's *The Clandestine Marriage*, a comedy of manners first performed in 1766. The passage (act 2, scene 2) is the following:

Lord Ogleby: [...] Hot rolls and butter in July! I sweat with the thought of it. What a strange beast it is! [...]

Canton: C'est barbare.

Lord Ogleby: He is a vulgar dog, [...].

p. 195, l. 12: *Mafra*: The Mafra Palace is a monumental Baroque and Italianized neoclassical palace-monastery located in Mafra, 20 miles away from Lisbon. It was a popular destination for members of the royal family who enjoyed hunting in the nearby game preserve. During the reign of King D. Joao VI the palace was inhabited for a whole year in 1807 and encouraged a partial renovation of the building. However, with the French invasion of Portugal in 1808, the royal family took some of the best pieces of art and furniture in the building with them to Brazil.

p. 195, ll. 20–1: *'ils se divertissent moult tristement'*: Mrs Baillie must have taken this French quote either from Froissard or after reading *Miscellaneous Works of the Late Philip Dormer Stanhope, Lord Chesterfield: Consisting of Letters to his Friends never before Printed, and Various Other Articles [etc.]*, in 3 vols (Dublin, 1777). In vol. 3, p. 89, letter 81 [written in 1763], Lord Chesterfield writes:

'Il se fait à toutes nos manières comme si elles lui étoient naturelles, et pourtant Dieu fait qu'elles font bien différentes des siennes. Il plait à tout le monde, mais pourtant au fond, il doit se divertir, comme dit Froissard, moult tristement à la mode de notre pays.' (French)

'He adapts to all our customs as if they were natural to him; however, God makes them appear rather different from his own. He pleases everyone; however, deep inside, he must have fun, as Froissard says, in a very sad manner according to the fashion of our country.'

p. 197, ll. 14–16: *The two princesses ... the late infant of Spain*: D. Maria Teresa de Bragança (1793–1874) was a widow of her first husband, the Spanish Infante Don Pedro Carlos de Borbón. The other sister who Mrs Baillie saw was very probably D. Maria Francisca de Assis de Bragança (1800–34).

p. 197, ll. 21–3: *Don Alfonzo ... fraternal cruelty*: D. Afonso VI (1643–83) reigned in Portugal from 1656 to his death. He was deposed by his brother, the future King D. Pedro III, who first exiled him to the Azores and then kept him in confinement in his own rooms at the Palace of Sintra for nine years, until he died.

p. 197, l. 26: *Sebastian*: Mrs Baillie is most probably referring to King D. Sebastião I, who reigned in Portugal from 1557 to 1578.

p. 200, l. 1: *Friseur*: 'hair-dressing' (German).

p. 201, ll. 7–8: *corporal Trim's poor 'brother Tom'*: a leading character of Laurence Sterne's *The Life and Opinions of Tristam Shandy* (1760–7).

p. 202, ll. 3–6: *Ferdinand of Spain ... the restoration of the inquisition of that country*: Fernando VII (1874–33), King of Spain in 1808 and again between 1813 and 1833, restored the Inquisition in January 1815 after José I (Napoleon's brother) had dissolved it during his short reign in Spain.

p. 204, l. 14: Malvolio: The antagonist in Shakespeare's comedy *Twelfth Night*.

p. 205, ll. 7–9: *the poet informs us ... Johnny Gilpin's wife*: In 1782 the poet William Cowper made a comic ballad based on the exploits and adventures of a real-life character, John Gilpin (eighteenth century), entitled *The Diverting History of John Gilpin*. It had been anonymously published in the *Public Advertiser* but was later included in Cowper's *The Task* (1785).

p. 205, l. 12: drover: somebody who transports or guides livestock or cattle.

p. 206, l. 5: *Rubens*: Peter Paul Rubens (1577–1640) was a Flemish painter whose female naked figures were characteristically sensual and generously fleshed.

p. 207, l. 2: *The Viscondessa de L—*: Mrs Baillie is probably referring to the Viscondessa de Lourihã, i.e. D. Domingas Isabel de Noronha, married to the former Colonel Manuel Bernardo de Melo e Castro. This viscontessa who is so praised by Mrs Baillie is thought to have been able to converse with the author in English, as she was educated by an English governess. See Afonso Eduardo Martins Zuquete's edition, coordination and compilation of *Nobreza de Portugal* (Lisboa: Enciclopédia, 1960–61).

p. 212, l. 23: *Telemachus*: Fenelon's *Les aventures de Télémaque* (1699), the most famous of his plays, is considered to be a subtle attack on the policies of King Louis XIV.

p. 214, l. 10: 'Pays de Cocagne': Cockaigne or land of plenty, an imaginary paradise, a utopia where humans live in permanent happiness and leisure and give free rein to their instincts.

p. 215, ll. 7–8: *the order of St. John*: The Sovereign Military Hospitaller Order of Saint John of Jerusalem of Rhodes and of Malta, heirs to the Knights Hospitaller.

p. 216, l. 25–p. 217, l. 5: *and that in a very few years ... the justice of these opinions*: The political crises in Spain and Portugal and the French occupation of both colonial powers in 1808 encouraged the aspiration for independence in South and Central America. The clashes between both countries and their respective colonies increased until they became armed conflicts from around 1810 onwards, especially during the 1820s. The independence of these new countries was encouraged by Britain, hence Mrs Baillie's support expressed in her letter.

p. 217, ll. 16–18: *The Prince Regent at Rio ... with the King his father*: When King D. Joao VI finally returned to Portugal in the early 1820s the majority of the privileges previously granted to Brazil were suppressed, a fact that provoked the irate reaction of the nationalists. D. Pedro (1798–1834), the regent in Brazil, allied with the nationalists and supported the Constitutionalist movement that led to the peaceful Revolution of Porto in 1820. He was pressed by the Portuguese court to go back to Portugal, but he refused to do so. His post of regent was taken from him and he was left with the status of a mere representative of the Portuguese court in Brazil. When he learnt this, on 7 September 1822, he exclaimed: 'Independence or death!' He was officially declared Emperor of Brazil on 12 October 1822 and crowned on 1 December.

p. 217, ll. 24–5: *convent of the Necessidades*: At the time of Mrs Baillie's stay in Portugal it was still a convent – and provisionally an assembly hall for the cortes – but during Queen D. Maria II's reign it was converted into a palace (Palácio das Necessidades) and used as the official residence of the kings of the Bragança dynasty.

p. 218, l. 13: *Punchinello*: A comical character derived from the *commedia dell'arte* of the seventeenth century and also known as Punch in English.

p. 220, l. 6: *Batalha*: Mrs Baillie is referring to the spectacular Monasterio de Batalha (in the town of Batalha, in the centre of Portugal), an excellent example of late Gothic architecture.

p. 222, l. 15: *Corregio*: Antonio Allegro da Correggio (1489–1534) was an Italian Renaissance painter of the Parma school who developed his vigorous and sensual painting in the court of the Farnese in the sixteenth century.

p. 222, l. 15: *Michael Angelo*: Michelangelo Buonarroti (1475–1564), Italian architect, sculptor and painter of the Italian Renaissance. He is best remembered for his sculptures of the Pietás, Moses and the painting of the ceiling of the Sixtine Chapel (as commanded by Pope Julius II), among other numerous works.

p. 225, ll. 11–12: *the Gray or Rundel of Lisbon*: Both Gray and Rundel & Bridge were very prestigious goldsmiths, silversmiths, jewellers and medalists in nineteenth-century London. Rundel & Bridge were made suppliers for the royal family in 1797 and held the Royal Warrant until 1843. They were the official jewellers for Kings George III, George IV, William IV and Queen Victoria. For more information, see *Royal Goldsmiths: The Art of Rundel and Bridge 1797–1843*, by C. Hartop, et al. (London: Adamson, 2005).

p. 229, l. 5: *Saint Antonio*: Santo António de Lisboa or Santo António de Padua was born Fernando Martins de Bulhões in Lisbon in *c.* 1191 and died in Padua in 1231. He was a Catholic priest and friar of the Franciscan order. He is widely venerated in Portugal and her ex-colonies. He is usually invoked for the recovery of lost things or people.

p. 231, ll. 3–5: *The Portuguese are ... people are of Seville*: Mrs Baillie seems to be referring to the popular sayings 'Quem não tem visto Lisboa, não tem visto cousa boa' ('He who has not seen Lisbon has not seen beauty') and 'Quien no ha visto Sevilla, no ha visto maravilla' ('He who has not seen Seville has not seen a wonder').

p. 231, l. 15: *'Adam alive again'*: No further information has been found on this satirical work that Mrs Baillie mentions. However, the three reviews of Mrs Baillie's travel account refer to it, albeit offering little extra information. These reviews are the following, in chronological order of publication: an anonymous review in the *London Literary Gazette and Journal of Belles Lettres, Arts, Sciences* (1825), pp. 7–8, where the book is described as 'full of feminine vivacity' (p. 7); an anonymous review in *The Modern Traveller. A Popular Description, Geographical, Historical, and Topographical, of the Various Countries of the Globe. Spain and Portugal*, vol 2 (London: James Duncan, 1826), p. 293, where we are informed of the price of the book (15*s*); and a repetition of the same review, this time signed by Josiah Conder, in the *Eclectic Review*, 25 (January–June 1826), pp. 91–4. All of them quote the author's allusion to 'Adam alive again'.

p. 233, ll. 19–23: *'La Festa da Rosa' … from Rossini*: Mrs Baillie is referring to 'La festa della Rosa', a comical melodrama whose music was composed by the Italian Carlo Coccia (1782–1873) and whose libretto was the work of the Italian Gaetano Rossi (1774–1855). It was performed at San Carlo theatre, Lisbon on 13 August 1821. For more information, see *O real theatro de S. Carlos de Lisboa desde a sua fundaçao en 1793 até á actualidade, Estudo histórico*, by F. da Fonseca Benevides (Typographica Castro Irmão, s. n. 1883). In *Harmonicon, A Journal of Music, Vol. 3, Part 1, Containing Essays, Criticisms, Biography and Miscellanies* (London: Samuel Leigh, 1825), p. 194, we find a review signed by William Ayrton, who speaks of the performance of the opera in Lisbon: 'After Mercandante's Elisa, a piece now to these boards, was produced, composed by Signor Coccia at Lisbon, entitled, La Festa della Rose, in which the contrail' [*sic*], Giuditta Favini, performed with great success. The music of this opera is full of pleasing effects, particularly a buffo-terzetto.' Using practically the same terms, Friedrich Rochlitz penned a review on Favini's performance in 'La Festa de la Mosa' [*sic*] in *Allgemeine musikalische Zeitung*, 27 (Leipzig: Breitkopt und Härtel, 1825), p. 251.

p. 233, l. 24: *Rossini*: The Italian Gioachino Rossini (1792–1868) is one the most popular composers of opera in history and therefore one of the most influential ones in his time. His most famous opera was *Il barbiere di Siviglia* (1816).

p. 234, l. 13: *Favini*: Italian mezzo-soprano, prima donna in numerous Italian operas of the time. She was known as Giuditta Favini or Giuditta Favini-Fasciotti. According to M. Moreau's *O teatro de S. Carlos: dois seculos de historia,* 2 vols (Lisboa: Hugin Editores, 1999), vol. 2, pp. 1387–406, Favini-Fasciotti performed regularly in Lisbon from 1815 to 1821.

p. 234, l. 26: *Beauharnois*: Napoleon's wife was Josephine Beauharnois Favini. According to Mrs Baillie, she could have accompanied the French expedition to Russia for the entertainment of the French court or of the French empress.

p. 236, l. 5: *St. Martin's summer*: This is popularly known as the last period of hot weather in late September. It comes from a legend in which St Martin is portrayed as a generous gentleman who shared his cloak on a cold day with a beggar by tearing it in two with his sword. In his honour, God grants the benefit of a few days' extra warm or hot weather at the end of the summer.

p. 239, ll. 11–15: *the Conde dos Arcos … exhibition of Corcunda principles*: The Conde dos Arcos (Marcos de Noronha e Brito, 1771–1828) was Portugal's last viceroy in Brazil. He was expelled by D. Pedro I, King of Brazil, and returned to Portugal. See Martins Zuquete's *Nobreza de Portugal*.

p. 241, l. 8: cachucha: Andalusian dance accompanied by castanets.

p. 241, ll. 9–10: *viola or Portugueze guitar*: Pear-shaped or tear-shaped guitar with six pairs of strings, attributed to artisan Luis Cardoso Soares Sevilhano. It gradually substituted the Spanish guitar in the accompaniment of fados.

p. 241, l. 24: *modinhas*: popular Portuguese songs of no fixed structure with sentimental or romantic lyrics.

p. 242, l. 6: *the tresses of* Berenice: According to Tycho Brahe (1546–1601), Berenice, the wife of Ptolomy III of Egypt, sacrificed her golden tresses to honour Aphrodite in gratitude for her husband's victory over the Assyrians.

p. 243, l. 17: *the English chapel*: St George's Church, built at Estrela and completed in 1822.

For Product Safety Concerns and Information please contact our EU representative GPSR@taylorandfrancis.com Taylor & Francis Verlag GmbH, Kaufingerstraße 24, 80331 München, Germany

Batch number: 08158361

Printed by Printforce, the Netherlands